master your

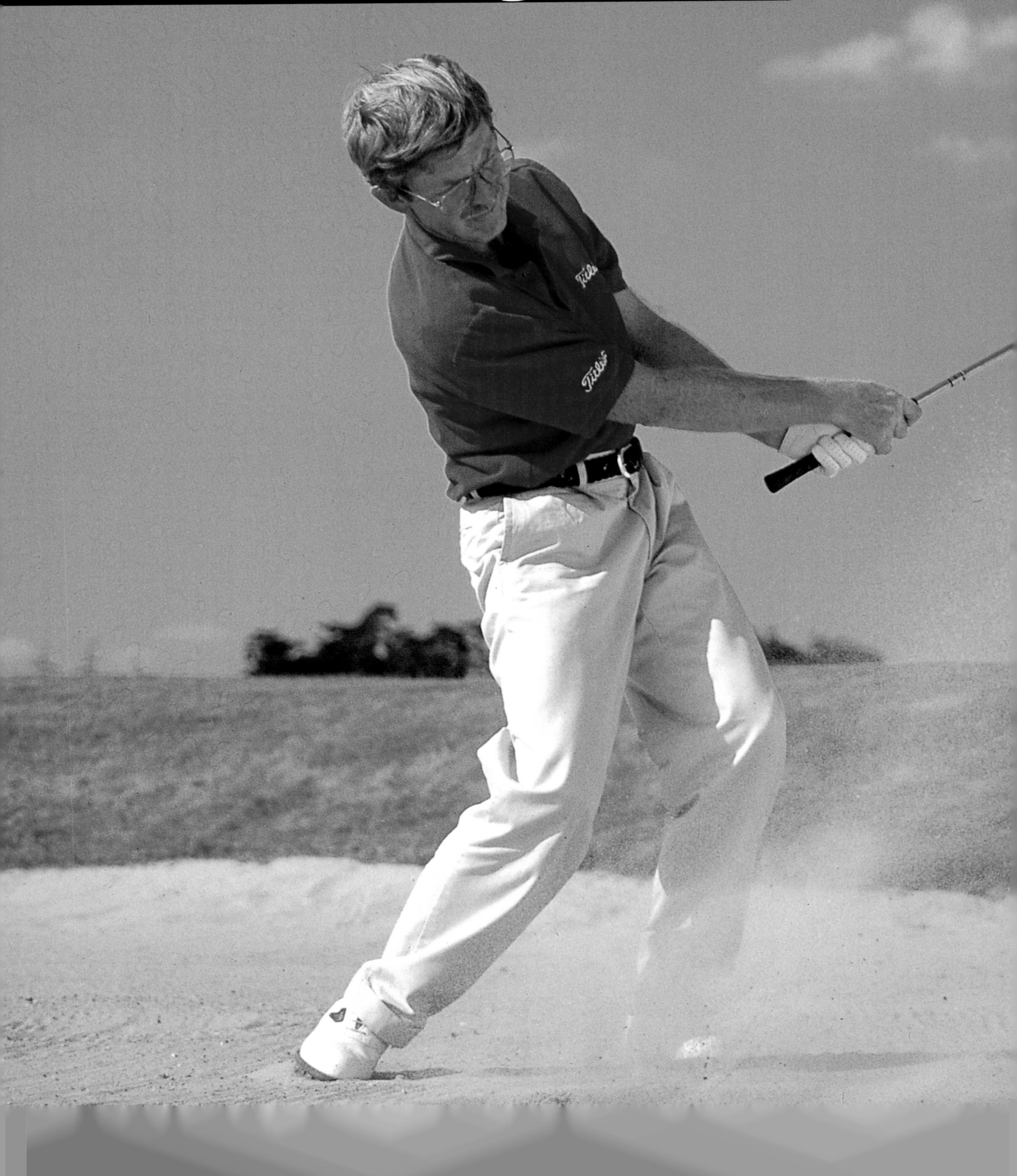

short game

by Tony Johnstone

MASTER YOUR SHORT GAME

First published in Great Britain in 1996
by Hamlyn an imprint of Reed Consumer Books Limited
Michelin House, 81 Fulham Road, London SW3 6RB
and Auckland, Melbourne, Singapore and Toronto

ISBN 0 600 58805 X

A CIP catalogue record for this book is available
at the British Library

Produced by Mandarin Offset
Printed and bound in China

ACKNOWLEDGEMENTS
We would like to thank Brocket Hall Golf Club in Hertfordshire for kindly giving us
permission to photograph this book on their wonderfully scenic course, and also for
allowing us to use their leisure facilities throughout the week. The staff, and in particular
the club professional Keith Wood, made us feel welcome at all times and their efforts
contributed greatly to the smooth running of this project.

Many thanks to Robert Walker for his efforts and photographic assistance during the shoot.
All photographs by Nick Walker

Art Director - Keith Martin
Editor - Adam Ward
Design - Darren Kirk
Jacket Design - Martin Topping
Production - Candida Lane

contents

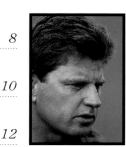

chapter 1
the three
fundamentals of the
short game   16

chapter 2
pitching   24

contents

putting   **112**

Preface
By Nick Wright

I'm often asked whether the star players who regularly contribute teaching articles to *Golf Monthly* play an active role in writing the material which appears under their name. All I can say, is that I make a point of insisting on it. Some players are more interested in passing on their thoughts and ideas about the game than others, but I have generally found that the better and more meticulous a player is on the golf course, the more time and effort he is prepared to devote to his activities off it.

So when I was asked to assist Tony Johnstone in the writing of this, his first instructional book, I can put my hand on my heart and say that I was absolutely delighted to do so. I've collaborated with Tony on numerous occasions over the past few years in his role as a contributing Professional for *Golf Monthly* and in that time, have found him to be the consummate professional, on and off the course.

Not too many people will be aware of this, but Tony has always fancied himself as something of a writer. His enthusiasm for the art of the written word is always reflected in his interesting and entertaining prose, and he is more than willing to spend time creating, discussing, photographing and proof-reading the instruction articles which appear under his name.

The same level of dedication also evident in all the work of the photographer, Nick Walker, who in my opinion is the best in the business when it comes to photographing golf instructional sequences. Meticulous almost to the point of being obsessive, the spectacular action photography you'll see in this book is testimony to Nick's steadfast refusal to click the shutter until he is absolutely 100 per cent happy with what he sees through the viewfinder. The results, I am sure you will agree, were well worth the time and effort.

I hope that you enjoy reading this book as much as we enjoyed putting it together.

Foreword by NICK PRICE

I first met Tony Johnstone in 1968 when I was 11 years old and he was 12. A gap of one year is often a major thing when you're that young, but Tony was a good head shorter than me – and he still hasn't caught up!

He had come to stay with me and my family in Harare, Zimbabwe, and it was the first time he had ever spent the night away from home. I remember his mother called every few hours to see if he was behaving himself.

We played golf the next day and it was then that I realised that Tony's size belied his courage. He has always played the game with an intensity that most of us have envied and in those days he had a temper to match, too. It was not uncommon to see him destroy two clubs, usually putters, in one round.

By the tender age of 12 he had already become something of a legend in his native town of Bulawayo. When I spoke to some of his golfing friends they all laughed: 'Oh, you've got Ovies staying with you ... ha, ha, ha!' Tony had apparently earned the nickname "Ovies" when he managed to hit a well-struck 3-wood straight into a greens' mower and followed this by shouting again and again, 'I want Ovies', which is local slang for wanting to play the shot again.

Tony made up for his lack of length as a youngster by developing an extremely sharp short game. As time progressed, he earned a new nickname, the "Sand Rat", because he spent so much time practising his bunker play. We all learned very quickly never to play Tony for money out of the sand. He is, I am sure, as good as Gary Player ever was.

I have been fortunate enough to be on six National teams with Tony and, although we didn't often play together as partners, we still claimed our fair share of scalps. He is, and always will be, an ideal team member whose tenacity and courage rubs off on all those around him – 'Never say die' should be his motto. I recall that many people doubted Tony's ability to succeed when he decided to turn professional, but I never once questioned it. He has since proved that with determination you can make it to the top; and no-one was happier than me when he won the prestigious Volvo PGA Championship in 1992.

Most importantly, though, Ovies has been and always will be one of my dear, dear friends. His ability to see humour in the darkest times is something that amazes me to this day. And even the fact that he married one of my old girlfriends has never hindered our friendship.

Introduction

By Tony Johnstone

I was introduced to golf when I was just eight years old and developed my taste for the game and my early playing skills on the courses near to my home town of Bulawayo in Zimbabwe, or Rhodesia as it was then known. My parents were always very keen for me to get out and play and I was also very fortunate that the local junior golf foundation was incredibly supportive, always organising plenty of competitions for the kids to play in.

The one, overriding memory of my childhood golfing days is how incredibly cheap it was. I remember it used to cost five cents for a whole day's play – and I mean a whole day. During the school holidays, my parents would drop me off at the course at 7.00 a.m. and pick me up in the evening after work. They used to give me one dollar, enough money for a caddie, lunch, drinks and a little bit of gambling money on the side, too. I would often play 54 holes, and still come home with change in my pockets. They were seriously fun times.

Looking back, I suppose one of the main reasons we used to play so much was that there was really nothing else to do. Our town had just two single-screen cinemas, so once you'd seen both films, that was it on the entertainment front for the week. Another contributing factor was the weather – Zimbabwe is blessed with one of the finest climates in the world for outdoor sports. During the summer months (and most of the winter), the sun shines virtually every day, there's very little wind and the temperature is very warm – absolutely perfect conditions for playing golf.

Although I played most of my golf locally, occasionally I would travel up to Harare and stay with Nick Price, then and still a good friend of mine. Even as a teenager, Nick was an immensely strong, strapping lad with huge forearms and he used to knock the ball miles past me off the tee. The years may have passed, but nothing has changed in that respect.

Being a slightly built youngster, I quickly learnt the importance of a sharp short game. Unable to carry the ball prodigious distances off the tee like some of my taller and

stronger friends, I frequently had to rely on my ability around the green and my putting prowess to score well. My swing was somewhat wild in those days, too, and very unorthodox: I held the club with a baseball grip, took the club away well outside the line on the backswing and, although my natural hand-to-eye co-ordination would often compensate for my somewhat less than orthodox technique, I still managed to miss a good many greens.

Although I'm glad to say that I have since developed a far more consistent long game, I learned that no matter how impressive I might be off the tee, I actually made my score with my short game – my ability to get the ball up and into the hole from around the green.

The world is full of golfers who can hit soaring drives, towering long irons and when on their game can tear any course apart. But when they start missing the green, these players struggle to keep their round together. Greg Norman was a good example of such a player when he first appeared on the PGA European Tour back in the early 1980s. Greg had a phenomenal long game, could putt like a demon and won many tournaments on those merits alone. But, by his own admission, his short game would let him down at key moments and he realised that unless he sharpened up his act around the green, he would never achieve the level of success his incredible talent deserved. In short, he would never win a major title. Greg went back to school and worked like a Trojan to bring his chipping, pitching and bunker play skills in line with the rest of his game. His hard work has since been rewarded with two Open Championship victories and many wins on the USPGA Tour. He is now one of, if not the, most complete players in world golf today.

Improving your own short game may not turn you into a major championship winner just yet, but it's the quickest way I know of lowering your scores. Whatever your skill level, if you can take the time to spend just an hour or so a week practising around the green, chipping in your garden or simply putting across your living room floor, you'll soon notice a major reduction in your handicap and, just as importantly, get so much more enjoyment out of this wonderful game we love to play.

the three fundamentals of the
1.short

game

1. ALWAYS ACCELERATE THE CLUBHEAD

I play with amateur golfers week in week out in the pro-ams which precede each tournament on the PGA European Tour and I see the same old faults occurring again and again. One of the most common, and most frustrating, is a lack of conviction demonstrated in the short game.

I have often said that a chip or pitch shot which finishes past the hole is one of the rarest sights in amateur golf. I believe the reason for this has nothing to do with the ability of the golfer in question to play the shot successfully, nor his understanding of the actual technique required to do so, but rather an ingrained fear of accelerating the club through purposefully.

Throughout this book I emphasize the importance of keeping the clubhead moving confidently through impact. I make no apologies for this because it really is the key to solid chipping, pitching, bunker play and putting technique. If there is indeed a secret to mastering the short game, then this is it.

Take a look at any of the world's finest golfers and you will see that they are all positive through the impact area. Watch José Maria Olazabal play a pitch shot, for example, and you'll be surprised at how he rips into the ball. When Seve Ballesteros splashes the ball out of a bunker, you will clearly see that he takes virtually a full swing and then zips the clubface confidently down and under the ball. Even on those delicate shots on and around the green, professionals still manage to keep the clubhead accelerating smoothly throughout the shot.

If you can just convince yourself to become a little more authoritative in this vitally important part of your game, I'm convinced that you'll knock at least five shots off your handicap and become a better player overnight.

Many of the world's top players now carry three wedges to help them deal with the variety of shots they come up against around the green. Adding an extra wedge to your bag will enhance your scoring ability.

2. CHOOSING THE RIGHT EQUIPMENT

Too many amateur golfers spend a fortune on a new driver in the hope of gaining an extra 10 yards off the tee, but pay scant attention to the real 'scoring' clubs in the bag – their wedges, short irons and their putter.

Think about it for just a minute. How many times will you use your driver during a round? I would say probably 12 or 13 times at most, but you'll use your putter twice if not three times as many as that. Finding a putter with which you you feel comfortable and confident should, therefore, be your number one priority.

Take a careful look at your wedges, too. You have to rely on them regularly to bail you out of trouble, so make sure that the clubs lie correctly and that when you look down at them you are happy and comfortable with what you see. If you don't like them, change them. Most manufacturers these days will sell sand wedges, pitching wedges and lob wedges separately from the rest of the set, so you don't necessarily have to stick with the same brand as the rest of your irons if you don't want to.

The extra wedge system

Many players on Tour nowadays, myself included, carry three wedges to help them deal with the wide variety of shots they face around

the green. A few players, John Daly and Sweden's Jarmo Sandelin for example, even carry four. Although I'm not suggesting you go to that extreme, I do recommend that you put a specialist lob wedge in your bag to complement your standard pitching wedge and sand wedge.

Let me explain why: my pitching wedge has 50 degrees of loft; flat out and in very still conditions I can make 120 yards. My sand wedge has 56 degrees and with a full swing I can hit the ball 90 yards. My lob wedge has 60 degrees and, if I catch the ball flush, I can just reach 75 yards. In other words, the lobber gives me one more full length pitching distance before I have to start shortening the length of my backswing and trying to 'feel' the shot.

Furthermore, as the name of the club suggests, the lob wedge is perfect when you need to throw the ball up high and land it softly. Rather than laying the face of your sand wedge right open and making a long backswing, the extra loft on your lobber enables you to keep the face square and make a shorter, safer swing, while still achieving the same result. Simple.

Finding the perfect putter

I must have experimented with virtually every possible style of putter known to mankind over the past 15 years or so on Tour – blades, broomhandles, mallets, I've tried them all.

This, would you believe, is just a tiny sample of the number of putters I've used (and often abused) over the course of my career. Some I still use on the odd occasion whenever I feel that a change will improve my fortunes on the greens, but the majority are likely see out the rest of their days in my garage, on top of my wardrobe or under my bed.

I have just one golden rule when it comes to choosing a putter – if it works, use it. Don't worry about whether or not you think it looks the part; if it gives you the inspiration and the confidence to get the ball into the hole on a regular basis, that's all that really matters.

It matters little what style of putter you use as long as it gives you the inspiration and the confidence you need to hole a lot of putts.

Selecting the right ball for your game

Pay a visit today to your local pro shop or specialist golf store and you'll find an absolutely staggering choice of golf balls. No matter what your skill level or shot pattern, the golf ball manufacturers have been working overtime in recent years to ensure there's a ball out there to suit your game: if you hit the ball high, there's a ball which will help you hit it lower; if you hit the ball low, you'll find one on the shelves to help you hit it higher. Just about the only thing the scientists cannot do yet is to produce a ball which flies long and straight no matter how badly you hit it. But I'm sure they're working on it right now, and as soon as they do, I'll be placing an immediate order!

Most professional golfers on Tour today use a ball with a rubber centre, a wound rubber outer and a thin covering of Balata, which is a soft rubber compound. Professional golfers and low handicappers, who are generally prepared to trade a little distance in exchange for increased control, prefer playing with this type of ball because its softer cover is more receptive to spin, making it easier for them to shape their approach shots, while enhancing their feel on those delicate touch shots around the green.

One of the main drawbacks to using a Balata ball, however, is its lack of durability. Because of the very soft cover, its surface is easily scuffed and damaged, which means that it is not an ideal choice of ball for beginners or higher handicap golfers who will mis-hit many shots. Even a top player, who strikes the ball out of the centre of the clubface, will find that this ball will begin to show signs of wear and tear after three or four holes and will therefore need replacing. I even know of some Tour players, Bernhard Langer and Ian Woosnam for example, who use a new ball on each hole.

At the opposite end of the scale from the Balata, there's the two-piece Surlyn ball, designed specifically for its longevity and distance. This type of golf ball has a solid rubber centre and a tough Surlyn cover, which

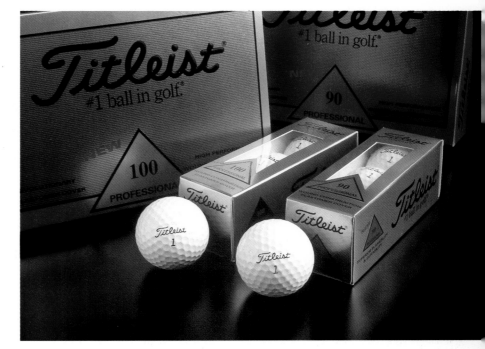

The two-piece Surlyn-covered golf ball (above left) generally provides more distance and lasts longer than the softer three-piece Balata ball (above right), which is more receptive to spin and therefore offers more control on full shots and improved touch and feel around the green.

is resistant to spin and therefore allows the ball to fly further. If distance off the tee is your main priority and you are happy to forsake a slight loss of control and feel around the green, then this could be the ideal golf ball for you.

Choosing a golf ball for your game, as you've probably gathered, basically comes down to deciding whether you want distance or control, or varying combinations of both. As well as the three-piece Balata and the two-piece Surlyn golf balls, there are plenty of other balls in between offering various combinations of distance, control and durability. I suggest that you experiment with them all until you find one that suits your individual requirements.

3. REGULAR PRACTICE

Below: Greg Norman is known for his powerful driving, but the statistics prove that he still relies on his chipping and putting to make his score. Top right: Practise those awkward shots and don't be afraid to experiment. You may have thought that you could only use a wood for hitting long shots, but it's an excellent choice of club when you find your ball lying tight against the fringe. It's up to you to see what kind of ingenious methods you can come up with for getting up and down in two from tricky situations.

Watch any of the world's top players go through their practice routine at a tournament and you'll notice that all of them spend as much time working on their short game as they do beating balls on the range, rehearsing the mechanics of their full swing. Whilst a solid long game is undoubtedly a major asset for anyone who makes his or her living playing golf, the world's top players are also well aware that, out on Tour if they should miss the green, it's the ability to get the ball up to, and into, the hole which leads to consistently lower scores and thus bigger pay cheques.

If you require further proof, take a look at the statistics. On the USPGA Tour in 1995, Greg Norman, who is probably the straightest and longest driver of the ball in the game today, hit just 13 out of 18 greens in regulation during an average round. This means that even the world's number one golfer has to chip and putt to save par at least four or five times during a round to make his score.

Unfortunately, you won't develop a deadly short game simply by reading this book – if only it were that simple. Technical advice, although certainly of great use, is still no substitute for regular practice when it comes to developing your touch and confidence around the green. A sharp short game is a combination of technique and feel; without good imagination and a feel for distance, the best technique in the world becomes redundant. And, of course, vice versa.

Here are a few pointers on how to get the most out of your practice sessions.

Regularly review your basics

Always make sure that your practice sessions have some form of structure. Start with the basics. Rehearse your set-up so that settling into the correct address position for each shot becomes second nature to you. In addition, follow the example set by the top players and review your fundamentals on a regular basis – each week if you have the time. Don't forget that nine out of ten problems with your game can be traced back to faults at address and that applies to the short game, too. Believe me, it's easy to slip into bad habits without realising it, but it's even more difficult breaking them, so do yourself a favour and never underestimate the importance of good fundamentals. I guarantee you that the results will be well worth the effort in the long run.

Learning the feel factor

Constantly chipping or pitching to the same pin position every time may be great for grooving your action, but it does nothing to nurture your sense of feel around the green. Whenever I'm working on my short game, I make a point of hitting to different targets. I find that varying the length of my backswing to hit one short, one medium and one full length chip, pitch, putt or bunker shot enhances my overall ability to gauge distance and visualise the shot.

Practice isn't just about rehearsing your technique, it's also about experimentation. Specifically, try varying the position of the ball, opening or closing the clubface, swinging slower and faster – make a note of how the changes affect the flight and roll of the ball and the overall shot. You'll soon develop a feel for what works for you and what doesn't!

Practise the trouble shots

Don't delude yourself by giving yourself a perfect lie around the green each time, either. During an average round of golf you have to play out of rough, from bare lies, off pine needles, leaves, out of divots, from severe slopes and up against the fringe, so make time in practice sessions for a few of those 'ugly' shots. That way you'll at least have an idea of what to expect when you come up against a similar situation out on the course. Be prepared.

Make practice fun and set yourself achievable goals

Practice can and should be enjoyable, but if you find it's becoming just a little monotonous, why not make it more interesting by playing games against yourself or perhaps challenging a like-minded friend? For example, find a quiet area of the course, throw down ten balls about 30 yards from the green and see how many times you can get up and down in two. From this kind of pitching range I would be looking for a success rate of at least 80 per cent, so make that your long term target. As your pitching skills improve, move back to 40 yards, then 50, then 60. Then

do the same with your chipping and bunker play. Adding a greater competitive element to your practice routine will improve your concentration and make the whole session more enjoyable and productive.

If you're new to golf or a high handicapper this may all sound a bit daunting. If so, start by seeing how many balls you can get within 20 feet of the hole or how many times you can get up and down in three shots. Then set yourself more demanding and realistic goals as you gain in confidence and skill.

When you're practising your bunker play it's a good idea to draw lines in the sand in order to remind yourself that while the clubface must aim at the target, you need to set up slightly open and swing the club back on the line of your feet and shoulders, not along the ball/target line.

Invest in a short game lesson

Most amateur golfers I know will happily approach their local club pro for advice on the long game, but they wouldn't dream of booking up a short game lesson. What an absolute waste of a golden opportunity to lower your handicap! If you're struggling with your bunker play, for example, don't carry on each week in the vain hope that you'll somehow manage to

avoid hitting the ball into the sand. Deal with the problem. I guarantee that if you spend just half an hour or so working on your bunker play technique under the watchful eye of a qualified PGA professional, you will eradicate forever your fear of the sand – and that piece of advice holds true for any aspect of the short game that you may find intimidating.

2.pitc

hing

THE BASIC
PITCH SHOT

A mini version of the full swing

In my opinion, the pitch shot is the most under-practised shot among club golfers. While most amateurs will at least throw a few balls down on the practice putting green or onto the carpet at home and work at some time on their putting or chipping, the pitch shot generally goes unnoticed in the practice regime.

For that one simple reason, too many club golfers approach this shot with trepidation instead of confidence, normally resulting in a less than impressive attempt at playing the shot, and an even less impressive outcome.

The pitch shot is a miniature version of the full swing. There's no major change as far as the actual swing technique is concerned, but because you are looking for accuracy instead of power, you

When setting up to play a standard pitch, choke down on the grip, adopt a fairly narrow, open stance and ease your weight slightly onto your left side.

need to make some adjustments to your set up to help you control the distance you hit the ball.

Start by narrowing your stance a shade and setting up with your weight just favouring your left side. Now open up your stance so that your feet and hips are marginally open (aiming left) to the target, while your shoulders remain square. Finally, choke down an inch or so on the grip of the club, thereby reducing the amount of clubhead speed you can generate and giving you a feeling of control and confidence over the shot.

Just as I would do in the full swing, I move the club away from the ball with my hands, arms and upper body working in unison. The feeling I focus on, and I believe it's a good one for you to concentrate on, too, is of my left arm staying connected to my chest in the early part of the backswing until the upward hingeing of my wrists causes it to naturally move up and away from my body. I allow my weight to transfer naturally across to my right side exactly as I would do if I was playing a full iron shot.

"Because of the inconsistencies in their long game, most club golfers will face more pitch shots in a round of golf than the average professional. Take the time to practise this area of your game on a regular basis and you'll be amazed at how quickly you can lower your handicap"

STARTING DOWN

Don't forget your legs

When you're pitching from fairly close range, the emphasis is on accuracy rather than power, but that doesn't mean you shouldn't use your legs in the shot. On the contrary, I like to 'feel' the shot with my legs just as much as I do with my hands and arms. Static or 'dead' legs often result in the hands and arms becoming overactive in the swing, which can

Most amateur golfers fail to get the ball up to the hole when they're pitching from close range, so commit yourself to the shot and always accelerate the clubhead at impact.

Think positively. From within 80 yards or so of the green, most Tour professionals expect to get up and down in no more than two shots. Make that your objective, too.

lead to your trying to scoop the ball in the air or having to wrap your hands over quickly at impact in an effort to square the clubface. The pitch is a synchronised blend of upper and lower body movement, NOT just a hands and arms shot.

As I mentioned in the very first chapter, accelerating the clubhead through impact is probably *the* most important key to a razor sharp short game and nowhere is this more important than with the pitch shot. In my experience, problems arise when golfers take too long a backswing and then, lacking either conviction or confidence, decelerate the clubhead through the hitting area resulting in failure to get the ball up to the hole consistently and numerous mistimed, badly struck shots.

"Although the premium is on accuracy with a pitch shot, you still need to use your legs. Static or 'dead' legs will result in the hands and arms becoming too dominant in the swing. Remember, the pitch is a synchronised blend of upper and lower body movement, NOT just a hands and arms shot"

THE BASIC PITCH SHOT

Take a narrow, open stance, ease your weight onto your left side and choke down on the club.

Move the club away using a combination of your hands, arms and upper body.

Stay down through the shot and allow your weight to transfer smoothly onto your left side.

Accelerate confidently through impact into a relaxed and well-balanced finish position.

To produce a more penetrating pitch shot, set up with the majority of your weight on your left side, play the ball back in your stance and push your hands forward to close the clubface.

"A real wind-cheater, the punch shot is perfect for keeping the ball low and out of harm's way in blustery conditions. For a piercing flight, focus on keeping your hands well ahead of the clubhead at all times in the downswing, through the hitting area and into your follow-through"

BEAT THE WIND WITH A PUNCH

Once you've mastered the basic pitch, your next step is to learn how to vary the flight of the ball by making minor changes to your set-up. The ability to 'work' the ball will enable you to deal with the wide variety of obstacles and weather conditions you'll come up against. Let's start by looking at the punch shot.

This produces a low, penetrating flight, which is particularly useful when you want to hit the ball under the branches of a tree, say, or simply for combating windy conditions.

Make the following adjustments at address: firstly, push your hands forward a touch to deloft the clubface and, secondly, ease your weight onto your left side and put the ball back in your stance, opposite your right instep.

Now when you make your swing, instead of allowing your weight to shift across onto your right side as you would normally, keep it fixed on your left side throughout the shot.

This will ensure that your hands stay well ahead of the clubhead and the ball through impact, making it easier for you to concentrate on the feeling of 'punching' the ball forwards.

One final consideration is that the lower trajectory produces significantly more roll on landing, so take this into account when you're trying to visualise the shot in your mind.

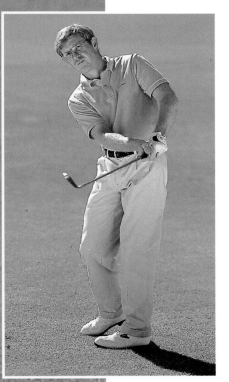

An abbreviated follow-through position indicates that the hands have led the clubhead all the way through impact. Try to finish like this, with low hands and with the clubhead held out in front of you.

"When you open up the clubface and cut across the ball you lose distance, so always remember to hit the high-flyer harder than a normal pitch shot, otherwise you'll find yourself coming up well short of the green"

Setting up open to the target with your weight slightly favouring your right side will push your hands back behind the ball, adding loft to the clubface.

With your shoulders controlling the rhythm of your swing, your hands and arms remain passive throughout, especially at impact.

THE HIGH FLYING
PITCH

When I'm within pitching range of the green I like to keep things simple if I can and use my basic technique to play the shot. However, there are times when this just isn't possible. For example, if I have some kind of obstacle or hazard to clear, or if the pin is cut really tight to the front edge of the green, as it is here, I need to be able to hoist the ball up in the air quickly and land it with accuracy.

For the high pitch, I set up open to the target, play the ball further forward in my stance and shift my weight slightly onto my right side. These changes automatically push my hands back behind the ball at address, effectively adding loft to the clubface and encouraging the out-to-in swing path required to cut across the ball at impact.

My shoulders dictate the rhythm of the shot, while my hands and arms remain fairly passive as I keep my swing as even-paced as possible. With the ball off my front foot it's easy to catch it thin, so the last thing I want is the clubhead rocketing through too quickly.

> "To achieve a high, floating trajectory, keep your swing as evenly paced as possible. Naturally, you must still accelerate smoothly through impact, but you don't want the clubhead zipping through too quickly when you're playing the ball off your front foot, where you could easily catch it thin"

When pitching from thick, heavy grass, give yourself a wide and secure stance. Remember also that the grass will wrap itself around the clubface, twisting it into a hooded position. Opening up the face of the club at address will ensure that the club returns to square at impact.

Make a confident swing and be aggressive at impact. Thick grass can stop a slow-moving clubhead stone dead, so always ensure that you swing through powerfully into a full finish position.

IN LONG FLUFFY GRASS
PLAY IT LIKE A BUNKER SHOT

Pitching out of long grass is never easy, even for top pros. You can never be quite sure exactly how the ball is going to react, but it normally comes out hot, rather like a mini-flyer. My first piece of advice is not to set your sights too high. You may get close with the occasional pitch from heavy grass, but if you can get the ball to within one-putt range of the flag first time, you've done well.

Secondly, always accelerate the clubhead confidently through the grass; decelerate and you're history. This may sound like rather obvious advice, but I've seen countless numbers of my pro-am partners try to 'baby' the ball out of thick grass like this, always with the same disastrous consequences.

My personal approach is to use my bunker play technique, by which I mean I open up the clubface and my stance just as I would if I was going to play a splash shot from sand. The only difference is that I normally select my pitching wedge to play the shot as it has a sharper leading edge than my sand iron and therefore will cut through the grass far more easily.

Another key is to steepen your swing. If you approach the ball at too shallow an angle, the grass will wrap itself around the clubhead, taking all the power out of the shot, so hinge your wrists earlier in your backswing and really concentrate on accelerating the clubhead purposefully down and through the grass.

You're going to need a little bit of luck to get it close from this kind of lie, but if you follow my advice you'll at least have a chance.

"Regardless of whichever technique you use to play this shot, the most important thing is to accelerate the clubhead through impact. Decelerate and you're history. Your priority is simply to get the ball out first time"

PINCH
THE BALL OUT OF A DIVOT

If I actually encountered a lie like this in a tournament, I think my initial reaction would be to grab the nearest rules official, get him to find the offending player, haul him over the coals and then slap him with a massive fine! There really is no excuse for leaving a fairway in such a terrible mess.

Normally, when you're playing out of a divot, the ground tends to be fairly firm, so instead of reaching straight for your sand wedge to play the shot, opt for a club with less bounce on the sole, a pitching wedge, say, or maybe a 9-iron. Bear in mind, though, that whichever club you choose, make sure it has enough loft to clear the lip of the divot, otherwise the ball will just pop straight up in the air.

The essential key to playing this shot is striking the ball first. Set up with the majority of your weight on your left side and with your hands ever so slightly ahead of the ball, which should be positioned back in your stance almost off your right foot. This should encourage you to hit down on the ball at a steeper angle than normal. Really feel as though you 'squeeze' the ball off the turf through impact, with your hands leading the clubhead all the way.

It's a bit of a lottery as to exactly how the ball will react, but it's certainly going to come out with plenty of top spin, so always take this into account and allow for the extra roll on the ball once it hits the green.

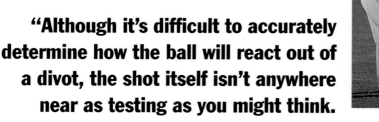

"Although it's difficult to accurately determine how the ball will react out of a divot, the shot itself isn't anywhere near as testing as you might think. Set up with the majority of your weight resting comfortably on your left side, push your hands just ahead of the ball...

...and keep your wrists nice and firm as you really 'squeeze' the ball forwards off the turf through impact, your hands leading the clubhead all the way through to the finish"

If you decide to use your basic splash shot technique to play this shot, set up open to the target with the face of your sand wedge square to the pin, then grip the club and swing back along the line of your feet. At the top of your back-swing the club should point to the left of the flag.

Just as you would do when playing a normal greenside bunker shot, swing back down to the ball along the line of your feet and splash the clubhead into the sand an inch or so behind the ball, throwing it out towards the pin on a cushion of sand.

SPLASH
OUT OF A SAND-FILLED DIVOT

I'll make no bones whatsoever about this one. Playing the ball out of a sand-filled divot is an absolute nightmare. Because greens staff at tournaments fill every unreplaced divot with sand at the end of each round, this is a shot which is far more likely to confront a touring professional than your average club golfer, but it's still worth knowing how to deal with the situation should it arise at any time.

First, trying to take the ball cleanly off such a lie is as difficult as chipping out of a bunker. It's a precarious shot that leaves a miniscule margin for error.

As far as I'm concerned, sand in a divot is exactly the same as sand in a bunker, so if I'm close to the green and can comfortably get the club to the ball, I'll treat this shot exactly as I would a straightforward splash from a green-side bunker. In other words, I open up the face of my sand wedge, open my stance and then swing along the line of my feet to ensure that I cut across the ball through impact, hitting about an inch or so behind the ball to blast it out on a cushion of sand towards the hole.

If all this sounds just too adventurous, or if you don't have quite enough faith in your bunker play technique to execute this shot successfully, providing the sand is fairly firm and you're not too far away from the green, putting the ball out of the divot is a safer and, all things considered, more sensible option.

"Sand in a divot is the same as sand in a bunker. If I'm close to the green and can get the club to the ball, I'll play this shot using my basic bunker play technique"

TONY'S TIP

Stay down and trust the loft on the club

I've lost count of the number of times I've seen amateurs try to scoop the ball up into the air when they've already got a very lofted club in their hands. A pitching wedge has about 50 degrees of loft, a sand wedge around 56 degrees and a lob wedge about 60 degrees, plenty of elevation to throw the ball comfortably up into the air without any extra, outside help from you.

Although you may think that scooping the ball will improve your chances of getting the ball airborne, it usually causes the exact opposite. When you get too wristy through impact you risk hitting behind the ball and fluffing the shot, or even worse, catching it right in the teeth with the leading edge of the clubface and sculling it right over the back of the green.

A simple but effective piece of advice is to stay down with the shot until it's obvious that the ball has left the clubface. In other words, let the clubhead do all the work.

TONY'S TIP

Use hips, chest and shoulders to judge distance

One of the reasons many amateurs fail to get up and down in two shots from within 100 yards of the green is an inability to control the distance of their pitch shots. If you take the time to work out and commit to memory the distances you can comfortably carry the ball when you make various length backswings, you'll be taking the guesswork out of your pitching.

Like all self-respecting Tour Pros, any time I'm within 100 yards of the green I'm looking to get up and down in no more than two shots. From this range I would be very disappointed if I couldn't land the ball within 10 feet of the pin to set up a makeable birdie putt. The reason that the world's top players are so accurate with their wedges is that they have developed a remarkable feel for distance by practising and playing golf virtually every day of their lives.

If you don't have too much time to spend working on your pitching, here's a good short cut to help you judge distance: when you next practise, make a note of how far you hit the ball when you swing the club back to hip, chest and shoulder height. If, say, you hit the ball 30 yards when you take the club back to hip height and 55 yards when you swing back to chest height, you'll know exactly what length of backswing you need to use when you face shots of a similar distance on the course.

Another good way to heighten your sense of feel is to practise hitting different length pitch shots. Set out targets 30, 40 and 50 yards away, for example, and hit to each in turn. Then try to land the ball between the targets. Constantly varying the length of your backswing will soon enable you to develop a feel for distance.

TONY'S TIP

Throw out a long iron and carry an extra wedge

Gary Player once said that over two-thirds of the shots in a single round of golf are played within some 60 yards of the green. He certainly has a point, but I believe that's a conservative estimate, especially for amateurs, who tend to throw away strokes by the handful when they find themselves close to the green.

For the majority of club golfers, the real scoring clubs are the short irons, not the long ones. If you carry a 1-, 2-, or even a 3-iron and struggle to hit it well, that's a waste of a club in my opinion. You'd be far better off leaving it out of your bag and replacing it instead with an extra specialist or lob wedge. Such an addition to your short game armoury will give you a few more options around the green, more versatility and a much better chance of seriously lowering your handicap.

Many golfers struggle to play pitch shots well because they often require a less than full swing. Unsure of their ability to control the ball from, say, a three-quarter length backswing they either swing the club too far back and then ease up through impact, or they rush the shot to get it over and done with. This tip will inject some rhythm and consistency to your pitching technique.

"If you're struggling to strike the ball with any degree of consistency on those awkward length pitch shots, try creating a mirror image with your backswing and followthrough"

"A smooth tempo is the key to spinning the ball and controlling its flight and distance. Rush the shot or quit on it through impact and you can forget any thoughts of hitting the ball close"

THINK OF A
MIRROR IMAGE
FOR BETTER TEMPO

A smooth tempo is vital if you want to pitch with any degree of consistency. Good rhythm will invariably lead to good clean contact, which is the key to spinning the ball and accurately controlling its flight and distance. If you rush the shot, lunge at the ball from the top or even quit on the shot, you'll always be struggling to get the ball close to the hole on a regular basis.

The best pitching tip I was ever given as a youngster was to keep my backswing and follow-through the same length. In other words, if I swing my arms back to chest height on my backswing, then I should swing them through to chest height in my follow-through. That's great advice because, not only does this ensure that your rhythm remains consistent, it also takes your mind off the striking of the ball.

3. chip

ping

THE BASIC CHIP SHOT

A real stroke saver around the green

The chip shot is basically a miniature version of the pitch shot, which, as I mentioned in the previous chapter, is itself an abbreviation of the full swing. The most noticeable difference between the two shots, though, is the width of my stance. As I'm only going to be making a fairly short backswing and follow-through, a wide, supportive base is unnecessary. In fact, you just can't play a delicate chip shot with a normal width stance. Just try it and see how awkward it feels.

If anything, setting up with your feet fairly close together will heighten your sense of feel and enable you to feel comfortable, relaxed and well-balanced over the ball at address. I

To guarantee a crisp, positive strike, set up with the ball well back in your stance and with your weight firmly fixed on your left side at address.

also like to play most chip shots with a slightly open stance, as I feel this enables me to accelerate the club comfortably through impact without my left hip or knee getting in the way.

As you can see here, I set my weight firmly on my left side and play the ball virtually off my back foot. This address position forces me to hit down on the ball, guaranteeing a crisper

and cleaner strike, while ensuring that my hands lead and accelerate the clubhead through impact, probably the most important key to consistent chipping.

Over the past few years, many of the top players have adopted a wristless form of chipping, where the stroke is controlled purely and simply by the rocking motion of their shoulders. The basic theory is that the larger muscles of the upper body are considered more reliable than the smaller ones in the hands and wrists, leading to more consistency under pressure.

While that method may work well for some, I'm afraid it's a little too wooden for me.

"Although I'm naturally a fairly wristy chipper myself, I recommend that you keep your hands as 'quiet' as possible during the shot. Unless you play regularly enough to develop good feel and touch around the green, too much wrist action can lead to any number of chipping problems"

FOR A CRISP, CLEAN STRIKE

Your hands lead the clubhead all the way

As far as my own technique is concerned, I've always been a fairly wristy chipper. I like to get my hands involved right from the start, and feel as though they control the shot from the length of my backswing to leading the clubhead firmly and confidently through impact. When I'm chipping well, I genuinely believe I can hole every shot from off the green. The feel and touch I've developed in my hands is a major contributor to that confidence.

With your weight on your left side, keep your hands and wrists firm as they lead the clubhead all the way through impact. Never allow the clubhead to overtake your hands.

The basic chipping technique is very simple. If you adhere to the key points and make time for some constructive practice, this part of the game will cause you few problems.

Once I've moved the club away, my key down-swing thoughts are simply to ensure that my weight remains firmly set on my left side as it was at address, and that my hands lead the clubface all the way through to the finish. I'm looking to keep my hands and wrists as solid as I possibly can through impact, as this will give me the best chance of achievng the slight downward strike required to nip the ball away cleanly.

I can't emphasise enough the importance of keeping your hands and wrists passive through the hitting area. It is the foundation to a good chipping action. Once you start flicking at the ball with your wrists or trying to scoop it into the air with your hands, you can wave the shot goodbye each and every time.

"I'm convinced that most amateur golfers would chip far more consistently if they kept their hands and wrists relatively passive throughout the shot and resisted the temptation to start flicking at the ball through impact. When this happens, it's all too easy to mishit the shot"

THE BASIC CHIP SHOT

Take a narrow, slightly open stance, ease weight onto your left side and choke down on the club.

Keep your weight set firmly on your left side as you make your backswing.

Make sure that your hands remain ahead of the clubhead at all times in the downswing and resist the temptation to flick at the ball.

Hold your finish position until the ball is well on its way towards the hole.

THE
PUTT-CHIP
METHOD
A no-hands approach

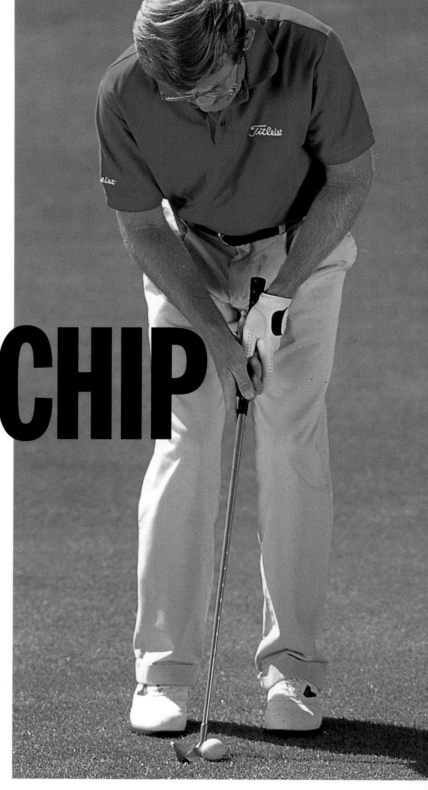

I've always considered myself a fairly good chipper, but when using my standard technique, which is basically a hands-and-arms stroke, if my timing was a bit out I was never really sure exactly how the ball would react once it left the clubface. Often it would take a couple of bounces, check and stop quickly on the green. Other times it would release and run on too far past the flag. Because of this inconsistency I decided to swap my wristy style of chipping in favour of a more shoulder-oriented method. I believe most amateur golfers who play just once a week or so would notice a remarkable improvement in their chipping consistency if they adopted this method.

Nowadays, any time I'm within about 15 yards of the green with a decent lie and a clear path to the pin, I'll chip using my putting technique. By that I mean I hold the club with my reverse overlap putting grip, adopt my normal putting stance and place my hands a fraction ahead of the ball, just as I would if I was addressing a putt on the green.

As you can see, I raise the club onto its toe slightly which serves two purposes; firstly, it steepens the shaft angle so that it recreates the lie of my putter, and secondly, because hitting the ball off the toe of the club will deaden the shot, I can be fairly aggressive, safe in the knowledge that the ball won't fly off the clubface too quickly.

Once I've set up, it's simply a matter of rocking my shoulders and keeping my head nice and steady to promote a crisp, positive strike. In playing the shot, I don't consciously think about my hands and arms at all. Although there is obviously some hand action involved, it is purely a reaction to the rocking motion of my shoulders.

Switching to this method has had a remarkable effect on my chipping. Why not see if it works for you, too.

"The real beauty of this method is its consistency. Whether I'm using a sand wedge or a 4-iron, I know that the ball will react off the clubface the same way every time – softly and with very little or no spin – making it easier to judge each shot"

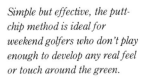

Simple but effective, the putt-chip method is ideal for weekend golfers who don't play enough to develop any real feel or touch around the green.

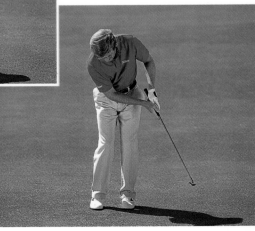

Allow the rocking motion of your shoulders to control the shot. Loft the ball over the fringe and let it run all the way to the hole.

CONQUER THOSE
YIPPY CHIPS
WITH A CACK-HAND GRIP

If you're a keen golfer you've probably heard of 'the yips', but perhaps thought that it was a term which only applied to putting. While the yips are, by and large, a putting affliction, they can, to a lesser degree, manifest themselves in the long game and the rest of the short game, too. For example, I know of a few top players who, after years of playing championship winning golf, suddenly found themselves in a position where they would literally 'freeze' over the ball at address, unable to start their back-swing. When they finally managed to move the club away from the ball, it was often a quick, jerky snatch lacking rhythm or control.

The yips in chipping can occur when the right hand becomes too dominant in the stroke. Instead of the hands and wrists staying firm throughout the shot, the right hand often develops a mind of its own and involuntarily flicks or stabs at the ball through impact, normally resulting in plenty of mistimed, fat and thinned chip shots.

If this sounds like you, experiment with chipping cack-handed by placing your left hand below the right on the grip. This automatically places your right hand in a less destructive position and, by levelling your shoulders at address, gives you the feeling of being able to control the shot with the rocking motion of your upper body, while your hands remain fairly passive.

Even if this method feels uncomfortable or awkward and you don't feel confident enough to use it out on the course for real, if nothing else chipping cack-handed serves as an excellent practice drill for grooving the sensation of 'quiet' hands in your chipping technique.

> "The chipping yips often occur when the right hand becomes too dominant and develops a mind of its own, flicking or stabbing at the ball through impact"

60

Using a cack-handed grip for chipping works on exactly the same principle as it does for putting. Placing your left hand below the right on the grip enables you to control the shot with the rocking motion of your upper body, and gives you the feeling of being able to lead the clubhead through to the target with the back of your left hand, while your right hand stays well out of trouble.

The laws of physics dictate that when the ball is above your feet it will fly downhill to the left when struck, so always aim a few yards right of the target at address. This type of lie also has the effect of bringing the ball nearer to your body. Give yourself plenty of room by standing a little more upright than normal and choking down on the grip.

LEAN INTO THE
SLOPE
When the ball is above your feet

With the introduction of more and more American-style stadium courses featuring built-in spectator mounding around the greens, this sort of shot is becoming more commonplace these days. Fortunately, playing from a tricky sloping lie like this isn't as difficult as it looks. It's a question of knowing which adjustments you need to make to your set-up to counteract the effects of the slope.

Firstly, make sure you are balanced and comfortable at address. When the ball is lying above your feet, as it his here, the cardinal error is to allow your weight to fall backwards onto your heels during the swing. To counteract this tendency, lean forward into the slope so that your weight rests on the balls of your feet.

Secondly, you should allow for the fact that this lie actually brings you nearer to the ball. To prevent you from getting too cramped at address, stand a little more upright and choke down a few inches on the grip to shorten the length of the club. These adjustments, combined with the fact that the ball is above the level of your feet, will force you to swing the club further around your body on a flattish swing plane.

One last but very important point: the laws of physics dictate that the ball will fly downhill to the left down the slope, so always remember to allow for this by aiming a couple of yards to the right of the target when you set up to play the shot.

You can see clearly here how the side slope affects the flight of the ball. Because of my closed address position, the ball starts out well right of the flag, but then moves down the slope in the air and comes to rest just a few feet from the pin.

Sit right down when the ball is
BELOW
YOUR FEET

When the ball is lying below the level of your feet, generally regarded as a more difficult shot than when it is above, you need to allow for the fact that the ball is further away from you and that it will always fly downhill to the right once it leaves the clubface.

As you can see clearly here, I've really flexed my legs, leaned forwards more from the waist and effectively lengthened the club by gripping it right at its end. I'm also standing a little closer to the ball than I would for a normal chip shot so that I can reach it more easily. However, when I do this I risk toppling forward down the slope, so to ensure that I stay balanced I set my weight right back on the heels of my feet and keep it fixed there as I play the shot.

Because the ball is now further away from you, you need to lean forward more from the waist, flex your knees and grip the club right at the end of the grip.

From this address position, accept that your backswing is going to be fairly wristy and slightly steeper than usual and remind yourself to swing even more rhythmically than you would on a normal shot. With such a miniscule margin for error here, the smoother and more rhythmical you can keep things the better.

"When I'm playing this shot a conscious thought of mine is to swing rhythmically, while keeping my body fairly 'quiet'. With such a tiny margin for error, the last thing you need is excess body action and quick, sudden moves"

This time the ball will automatically fly to the right in the air as it follows the slope, so always rememver to aim a few yards left of the pin at address to allow for this extra movement.

FROM AN
UPHILL LIE

You can always be aggressive through impact

Whenever the ball is lying on a slope, uphill or downhill, the key to playing the shot adeptly is to make a couple of amendments to your chipping technique so that your swing can follow the contours, not fight against them.

The first and most important of these adjustments is to align your spine at right angles to the slope in question. This will also set your hips and shoulders parallel to the ground, effectively recreating a flat lie. As you can see here, I've had to lean backwards slightly and this has shifted my weight back onto my right side. Once I've made these adjustments, I can simply go ahead and use my normal chipping technique to play the shot.

Secondly, it's an often overlooked fact that slopes will either add to or detract from the loft on the club. In this case, the gradient is effectively adding another 20 degrees, which means club selection needs careful consideration. Instead of using a wedge to play the shot, which will send the ball straight up in the air, it's often a good idea to take a club with a slightly straighter face, a 9-iron, say, or even an 8-iron.

Because of the severity of the upslope this is a shot where it pays to be fairly aggressive through impact. Knowing that the ball will always fly fairly high and stop relatively quickly on landing, you can confidently swing the club through into a new full finish position.

Keep your weight fixed firmly on your right side throughout the shot particularly as you hit down and through the ball. If you attempt to transfer your weight across to your left side in the downswing, you risk fluffing the shot completely.

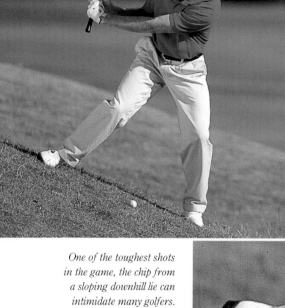

One of the toughest shots in the game, the chip from a sloping downhill lie can intimidate many golfers. The key to executing the shot competently is to set up with the majority of your weight on your left side at address, use a fairly lofted iron and then simply swing with the slope, ensuring that you keep the clubhead low to the ground through impact and well into your follow-through. Take a close look at my finish position and see how relaxed, comfortable and balanced I am. That's a sure sign of a smooth, unhurried, confident swing.

FROM A SLOPING
DOWNHILL LIE

Set your angles and then follow the contours

Just as an upslope will add loft to the club, so a downslope will always lose loft and, as a consequence, the ball will have a tendency to fly off low and fast. To counteract this effect, using one of your more lofted irons is often a good option as it will 'soften' the physical effects of the downhill lie and give you a little more height and, in turn, control over the shot.

As I mentioned on the previous page, setting your spine at right angles to the slope so that your shoulders and hips are parallel to the ground is the key to playing from a sloping lie. This time I tilt my spine forwards slightly so that my weight falls naturally onto my left side, and brace my left leg, exaggerating the flex to ensure that it remains solid and secure throughout, supporting my weight.

As far as the stroke is concerned, again it's just a case of swinging with the slope. Chipping from a downhill lie is arguably more difficult than from an upslope because it's easier to mis-hit the shot. To guarantee a crisp, clean strike, I concentrate on keeping the clubhead low to the ground in my downswing and well into my followthrough. This lessens the risk of hitting up on the ball too early and catching it too thinly.

THE
LOB SHOT

This is a shot that always impresses the crowds. They love to see the players really open up the clubface, send the ball straight up in the air and stop it softly right next to the flag. Entertaining stuff certainly, but the lob shot has given me more trouble over the years than any other around the green, mainly because until recently I'd struggled to find a method that I felt confident enough to use in tournament play. I must have tried 50 different techniques in an effort to find something that worked for me, but finally everything clicked into place after watching Seve Ballesteros practise these shots. What I noticed was how flexed he kept his knees and how low to the ground he positioned his body at address to ensure that the clubhead approached the ball at a shallow angle – and that really is the key to playing the lob shot successfully.

If I'm using a sand wedge, I open up my stance so that my feet, hips and shoulders are all aiming slightly to the left of the target, so when I make my normal swing along the line of

Contrary to what you may have thought, you don't need a steep, wristy swing to get the ball up into the air quickly. In actual fact, the key to playing the lob shot is creating a very shallow angle of attack – keeping the clubhead moving low to the ground to maximise the loft on the clubface.

70

To facilitate a shallow angle of attack into the ball, move the club away low to the ground and allow your wrists to hinge naturally in response to the swinging momentum of the clubhead. Resist the temptation to scoop the ball up in the air with your hands and instead simply rely on the loft of the clubface and your open address position to throw the ball up into the air quickly.

my feet, I cut across the ball slightly at impact. I also open up the face of the club before I grip it to increase the loft further and I also choke down an inch or so on the grip for extra control.

As I take the club away low to the ground, allowing my wrists to hinge naturally, my next thought is to accelerate smoothly through impact, making sure that the clubhead remains low to the ground in the follow-through. As you can see, I haven't tried to scoop the ball into the air with my hands, but simply relied on the adjustments I've made to my address position to create the shallow angle of attack into the ball.

Finally, a word about equipment. You can play this shot with a sand wedge, but it's far easier to use a 60 degree wedge or a lob wedge. The extra loft on the club means you can play the shot with the face square to the target and eliminates the need for any adjustments to your address position to get the ball airborne.

"Seve Ballesteros is the undisputed master of the lob shot. Notice here how his knees are still nicely flexed well into his follow-through and how he keeps his body low to the ground. This ensures that the clubhead approaches the ball at a shallow angle – and that's the key to playing the shot successfully"

Playing the ball back in your stance opposite your right toe and pushing your hands well ahead will keep your wrists out of the shot and maximise your chances of nipping the ball away cleanly.

CLIP THE BALL OFF A TIGHT
BARE LIE

The most important piece of advice I would give to any player facing this shot is to avoid using a club with a lot of bounce on the sole, such as your sand wedge. The last thing you want is the clubhead to ricochet off the hard ground, catch the ball half way up the face and thin it across the green into the next county! Unless you have to get the ball up in the air very quickly to clear a hazard or have very little green to work with, always play these shots with your pitching wedge or one of your shorter irons, as the sharper leading edge will give you more margin for error with the shot.

The next thing for consideration is your address position. Placing your hands well ahead of the ball, which you play back in your stance just off your right instep, will encourage the steep, downward strike that you need to play these shots well. Again, the wrists should remain firm throughout and, even more importantly, keep your head perfectly still. This shot requires precision. If your head moves from side to side you'll find it difficult to accurately judge your point of impact. The slightest error from this lie can have disastrous consequences!

"What's all the fuss about? It was only a 40-yard chip shot off a bare lie, across a downhill side slope to a pin cut right at the back of the green just a few yards from the water. Anyone could have knocked it to within four feet of the flag at the first attempt!"

THE LEFT-HANDED
ESCAPE

Hopefully you won't find yourself in this kind of precarious position too often, but if you do, here's a technique that will help you get the ball back in play first time.

Most players I see attempting to play left-handed, grip the club as they would to play a normal shot, with the right hand below the left on the club, and then flick at the ball with their wrists. They don't really have much control, if any, over the shot and often end up missing the ball completely!

Try my method by first selecting your sand or lob wedge. The larger-sized clubhead will provide more of a target to aim at

and more confidence as you stand over the ball. It's also much easier to play the shot with your left hand below the right using a split grip,

The left-handed escape shot is a great way of getting the ball safely back in play whenever it has come to rest awkwardly against the base of a tree trunk or some other kind of obstacle which prevents you from playing your normal shot. The split-grip method which I've devised especially for the shot allows you to give the ball a good thwack.

your hands well apart and your right arm slightly bent, while your left arm hangs straight down. It's also a good idea to push your hands forward slightly as this reduces the risk of hitting too far behind the ball and gives you the feeling of really being able to 'punch' the ball forwards.

This isn't the time for anything too fancy, so it's a probably wise to restrict your technique to a simple swing back and through. But even so, this grip still allows you to give the ball a good thwack with your left hand. As you can probably see here from the trajectory of the ball, I came very close to hitting our photographer, Nick Walker, who was standing only about 20 yards away. Although Nick wasn't too impressed with the new centre-parting I almost gave him, it just goes to show how effective this shot can be!

> **"This isn't the time for anything too fancy, so it's a good idea to restrict your technique to a simple swing straight back and through"**

CLEARING
HAZARDS
WITH CONFIDENCE

The importance of accelerating the clubhead is a continuous theme in this book, but it's crucial when you're facing a shot where your path to the green is blocked by some kind of hazard, in this case a large, imposing bunker.

Put your average club golfer in this position on the course and I'll bet that, more often than not, he'll hit the ball straight into the sand. It's a mental problem, of course, but one which is easily cured by a little rational thinking.

In my experience, most golfers make the mistake of taking too long a backswing and then, suddenly fearing that they're going to hit the ball too far, quit on the shot and duff the ball straight into the trap. The next time you find yourself facing a shot which makes you a little uneasy, slow things down. Take the time to survey the shot and work out where you think you need to land the ball to get it close. Rushing the shot simply to get it over and done with is a sure-fire route to disaster. What's more,

thinking constructively about your strategy will help you focus your mind on the positive elements of the shot rather than the negative.

"Reducing the length of your backswing will force you to be more positive through impact, thus improving your chances of clearing the hazard. Remember, it's nearly always better to be long than short, so play the percentages and err on the side of safety"

TONY'S TIP

Chip with all your clubs

Many top players advocate chipping with just one particular club, but I like to use anything from a sand wedge to a 4-iron, as I feel this gives me more versatility and a few more options from around the green.

I'm a great one for trying to keep things simple wherever possible. Instead of having to manufacture a variety of shots with just one club to suit specific situations, I can concentrate purely on one technique and then simply vary the club and the length of my swing to produce shots of different lengths and trajectories.

79

If you are experiencing difficulties with your chipping, take the time to visualise the shot in your mind before you play it. Picture yourself carrying the ball a yard or so onto the green and letting it roll towards the target. If you can 'see' the shot you'll stand a much better chance of playing it successfully.

TRY
SPOT
CHIPPING
To enhance your feel

When I'm working out in my mind how best to play a chip shot, nine times out of ten I'll be thinking about landing the ball a few feet onto the green and letting it roll the rest of the way to the pin. Once I'm happy with my assessment, I take the club which I feel gives me the best chance of playing the shot as I see it.

However, there's no point in picking out a landing area if you don't have the skill to hit the target accurately. The next time you work on your chipping, try this exercise to improve your feel. Pick out a spot of grass a yard or so onto the green and mark it with a tee peg or something that's easily visible. Now practice chipping to the tee peg or marker until you can consistently land the ball close to, or onto it, every time.

Once you're confident in your ability to do this, experiment by chipping to the same spot with a selection of other clubs and note the results. Not only will this drill improve your overall feel, it will also teach you the carry/roll ratio you can expect for every club in the bag.

"When I'm working out how best to play a chip shot, nine times out of ten I'll be looking to land the ball a few feet onto the green and let it roll the rest of the way to the pin. Then I choose the club which I believe gives me the best chance of playing the shot as I see it"

Although visualising a chip shot clearly in your mind before you play it will undoubtedly improve your chances of knocking the ball close to the pin, it's a waste of time if you then don't have the ability to play the shot as you see it.

4. bunk

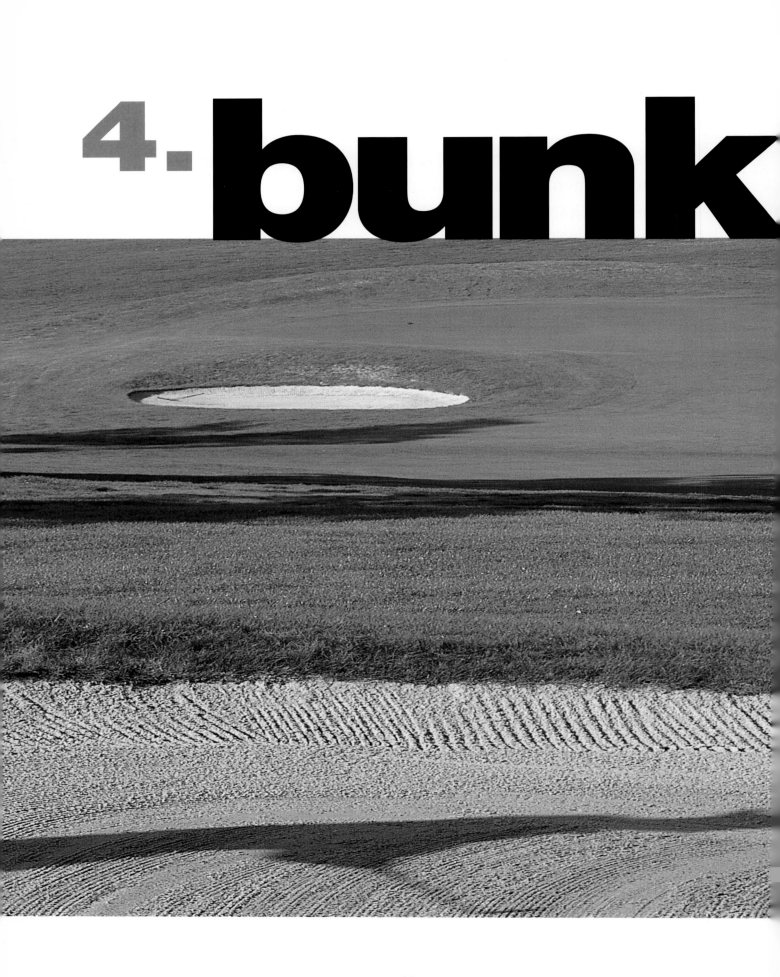

er play

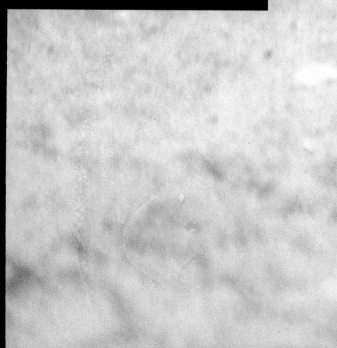

Many of you reading this will be surprised to learn that I love playing bunker shots. In fact, I'm sure that my positive approach to bunker play is the principal reason my 'sand save' statistics have made such impressive reading over the last few years.

Every time I step into a trap, I have a clear objective of what I am trying to achieve and can therefore approach the shot with confidence. Unfortunately, the reverse is true for many amateurs. Most club golfers would prefer to step into the ring and go 12 rounds with Mike Tyson than face the prospect of playing a bunker shot under pressure. With such a negative mental attitude, you're beaten before you start and stand almost no chance of playing a decent shot.

SAND PLAY
OVERCOMING THE FEAR FACTOR

You may have heard this before, but I'll say it again because it really is true – bunker shots are easy. Let me explain. Firstly, with a bunker shot you don't actually have to hit the ball. Your sand wedge has been designed specifically to slide smoothly through the sand without digging in too deeply. Taking a thin cut of sand, the club allows you literally to 'splash' the ball out. Secondly, there's more margin for error in a bunker shot than there is with any other shot in golf. Whether you hit one, two or three inches behind the ball, as long as you accelerate the clubhead confidently through the sand, you'll get the ball out of the bunker every time.

But before I get too far ahead of myself here, you must first fully understand the components which go into producing a good bunker shot, before you even think about becoming a sand supremo. So let's go to work on your splash technique.

Open up the clubf
then grip the cl

O f all the fundamentals to which
to adhere when playing a bunke
one is by far the most important. Try
a soft, controlled splash shot with a s
face is about as easy as trying to get b
a stone. To see why the sand wedge
when the face is open, take a look a
sole of the club is designed. You'll s
flange is set lower than the lea
Referred to as the 'bounce', it's this de
which prevents the club from diggir
sand and instead enables it to skim t

Now if you twist the clubhead ir
position, you'll see that the flange
sits in an even lower position than i
the face was square, in turn making
ier for the clubhead to enter and exit

Many amateurs realise that th
open up the face, but often go about it
way. For the club to work to its full
has to remain open throughout the sh
won't happen if you just grip the clu
and twist it open by turning your ha
this artificially open position the clu
naturally return square to the ball at

To guarantee that the face of
wedge stays open throughout the
swivel the face open with the thumb
of your right hand only, then go ahea
the club as you would normally.

THE BASIC
SPLASH SHOT

Set up correctly for sand success

For the basic greenside splash shot, and indeed any shot from the sand, your address position is absolutely crucial. Follow my routine to make sure you get it right.

Set up with your feet, hips and shoulders in an open position, aiming left of the pin, as if you were going to hit a shot about 30 feet left of the target. Make sure that you place the majority of your weight on your left side to promote a steep backswing, and that you position the ball slightly further forward in your stance than normal – a couple of inches inside your left heel is just about perfect.

With your hands placed directly above or even fractionally behind the ball, now open up the face of your sand wedge so that it aims straight at the target, *then* grip the club and shuffle your feet into the sand to give yourself a secure footing.

One last point: Remembering that the Rules of Golf strictly prohibit you from touching any part of the sand with the clubhead before you play your shot, pick out a small grain of sand about an inch or so behind your ball and hover your club directly above it. This will be your intended point of entry into the sand and you should now forget about the ball completely.

Make a steep swing and forget the pin

The takeaway is the most important part of the bunker shot, but it's also where most players go wrong. From this open address position don't, as many amateurs do, try to swing the club back inside along the ball/target line. That only leads to an exaggerated flat swing plane in relation to your open stance, a shallow attack into the ball and plenty of ugly fat, thinned and shanked bunker shots.

Forget about the pin and simply swing the club straight back along the line of your feet and shoulders, again as though you were going to hit the ball to the left of the target. Because I like to play bunker shots predominantly with my right hand, I make a conscious effort to hinge my right wrist earlier and more steeply than normal in the first stages of my backswing, as I find this puts me in a position where I can really attack the sand with a confident steep descending blow.

"When you're playing a basic splash shot your feet, hips and shoulders all aim to the left of the target, but the face of your sand wedge aims straight at the pin. Once you fully understand that you have to swing across the target line, you're well on the way to mastering bunker play"

THROUGH IMPACT

Accelerate and slap the sand with your right hand

Most amateurs fail to escape from bunkers first time because they 'quit' on the shot. Remember that you're not only propelling the ball out of the bunker, but a considerable amount of sand, too. Your technique needs to reflect this.

Never try to 'baby' the ball out of the sand unless, of course, you want to play your next shot from a similar lie. Having said that, the key to propelling the ball out of the bunker isn't to slam the clubhead into the sand as hard as you can, but to accelerate it through smoothly.

Once you've completed your backswing, think only of swinging the club back down to the ball on the same line along the line of your feet, not towards the target. Once again, you should forget the pin and simply imagine that you're hitting the ball left of the flag. I know

Swinging back down along the line of my feet and shoulders, I stay commited to the shot and really accelerate the clubhead through the sand, 'slapping' it with my right hand.

You can tell here by the direction in which my divot is pointing that my swing path is well outside the ball/target line. But because I aimed the face of my sand wedge at the target at address, the ball has flown straight at the target on a cushion of sand.

that some readers will be concerned that the ball will fly to the left of the pin, but don't worry. Because you aimed the face of your club at the target at address, that's exactly where the ball will go.

A feeling I like to concentrate on is of 'slapping' the sand with my right hand through impact, trusting the bounce of the sand wedge to prevent the club from digging in too deeply. I aim to hit about an inch behind the ball on a regular bunker shot, but for most amateurs I would recommend taking two inches of sand as this will give you a little more margin for error. As long as you accelerate the clubhead confidently, the ball will fly out on a cushion of sand towards the target every time.

"How far you hit behind the ball is down to personal preference and what suits you best. What is crucial, however, is that you keep the clubface in an open position throughout the shot and that you stay focussed on your point of entry into the sand until the ball is on its way to the pin"

THE BASIC SPLASH SHOT

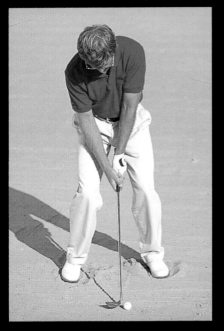

*Open your stance so that your feet,
hips and shoulders all aim to the left of the pin.
Open the clubface before you grip it and pick out
a grain of sand an inch or so behind the ball.*

*Keeping your weight on your left side, swing
back along the line of your feet and shoulders.
Hinge your right wrist earlier than usual to give
you the feeling of being able to hit down steeply.*

*Accelerate the clubhead smoothly and
confidently. Feel as though you 'slap' the sand
with your right hand through impact. Don't
make the cardinal error of quitting on the shot.*

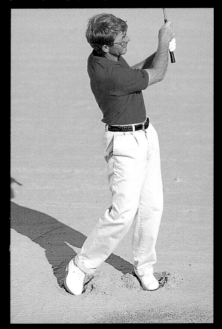

*My relaxed, balanced, fairly full finish position
shows that I've maintained my rhythm
throughout the shot and that that I've
accelerated the club smoothly through impact.*

ONLY AS A LAST RESORT
CHIP THE BALL
OUT OF THE SAND

I must admit that I would never in my wildest dreams contemplate chipping the ball out of the sand. Not ever. Not only is the margin for error too small for my liking, but also I'm confident enough to escape from any kind of trap with my normal splash technique.

At the same time, I'm aware that many golfers get very nervous in bunkers and that their fears increase when they are close to the pin with little or no lip to negotiate. Knowing that their technique is not up to scratch, the demons inside their head start working overtime to convince them that they're going to thin the ball right over the back of the green.

If this sounds like you, the best piece of advice I can offer is head straight to the practice bunker and work on your technique until you are confident of your ability to play the shot proficiently, whatever the circumstances. However, if you are going to chip the ball out, at least do it correctly; there's no point in taking what you believe to be the easy option and then making a real hash of it.

The main factor in executing this shot successfully is keeping the clubhead out of the sand. This is absolutely essential. The resistance of the sand can stop a

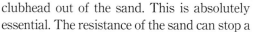

The key to chipping the ball out of a bunker is setting up in such a way as to promote the shallow attack you need to nip the ball off the top layer of the sand.

slow moving clubhead virtually stone dead in its tracks and if this happens you'll be lucky if you move the ball six feet. Instead, you should be aiming to 'clip' the ball off the top layer of sand with a shallow, almost wristless swing.

Set up square to the target as though you were going to play a normal chip shot, but this time spread your weight fairly evenly between your feet to encourage a shallow attack into the ball. This is one instance where a thinned shot is not too disastrous, so you can afford to play the ball a little further forward in your stance. Throughout the shot, keep the clubhead moving as low to the ground as possible, ensuring that your wrists remain firm. This will promote a shallow delivery of the clubhead and give you more chance of nipping the ball cleanly off the top of the sand.

"As a competent bunker player, I would never contemplate trying to chip the ball out of the sand unless I had absolutely no other option. However, if you don't have the same level of faith in your own ability to splash the ball out, this shot can be a real lifesaver"

93

UNPLUGGING THE
BURIED LIE

O f all the lies in a bunker, this is probably the one that amateurs fear most, but it's really not as bad as it looks. The first thing to remember is not to be too clever with the shot. Until you're confident of your ability to escape from this type of lie first time, simply getting the ball onto the green should be your priority.

Don't even think about trying to use your standard splash technique to play this shot – that just won't work. You need to move an awful lot of sand here to force the ball out, which calls for a totally different technique.

Instead of requiring the club to bounce through the sand as you would with a splash shot, this time you need the clubhead to dig in really deep and stay there. To ensure this happens you have to make a few adjustments to your address position. Firstly, close or hood the clubface slightly before gripping the club. This enables the leading edge of the blade, rather than the sole of the club, to make contact with the sand first. The only time I would even

"Feel as though you sling the club over your right shoulder in the backswing, then accelerate it down into the sand as if you were driving a nail down into the ground"

From a plugged lie your first priority is to give yourself a putt for your next shot and not another bunker shot. Follow the advice I've given you here and always err on the safe side. Don't be afraid to give the sand a good thump through impact.

contemplate playing this type of shot with an open face is if I had no green to work with and had no option other than to try and get the ball up in the air and stop it quickly to get it close to the pin. Secondly, square up your stance so that it's parallel to the target line and ease your weight onto your left side.

Once you've made these adjustments, pick up the club really steeply in your backswing, as though you were going to throw it over your right shoulder. Then, once you reach the top, simply accelerate the clubhead straight down into the sand about an inch or so behind the ball, as though you were driving a nail straight down into the ground.

"Judging distance accurately from a plugged or buried lie comes with experience, but it's worth remembering that the ball will always come out low and running with plenty of topspin"

Judging distance from this type of lie comes with experience, but one thing to remember is that the ball always comes out low with plenty of topspin, so you'll need to take that into account if you're looking to get the ball close.

Whenever the ball is buried or plugged the sand will create plenty of resistance through impact. Consequently, don't expect to be able to make too much of a follow-through.

I approach this shot in exactly the same way I would a lob shot from fringe grass, meaning that I do everything possible to make my downswing shallow and maximise the loft on the clubface through impact.

"Another trick to try once you've gained confidence is to work on keeping the clubface pointing upwards at the sky through impact. Feel as though the clubhead overtakes the hands while your right hand flips underneath the left as it slides right under the ball. Once you get it right you'll be amazed at how quickly you can fizz the face of the club under the ball and yet still have it travel only a few yards"

THE HIGH FLOATING SPLASH SHOT

Once you've grasped the fundamentals of the basic splash, your next step is to learn how to adapt your technique in order to play a wider range of bunker shots. For example, when you find yourself in a greenside trap with only a short distance to the pin and no green to work with, your only option is the high-floater which lands as softly as a butterfly with sore feet.

I love to play this shot, but I should point out that it's a specialist technique and should be attempted only once you've mastered the basic bunker shot. There's no point trying to run before you can walk.

I start by widening my stance, shuffling my feet lower into the sand and increasing the flex in my knees. I also open up my stance a fraction more than I would to play a run-of-the-mill splash shot from the sand and I choke down a few extra inches on the grip. All of this helps reduce the distance you can hit the ball and gives you the confidence to really accelerate the clubhead under the ball, knowing that the increased loft on the clubface will propel it upwards rather than forwards.

From here, I swing back along the line of my feet as normal, but I also try to cut across the ball slightly, holding the face of my sand iron open through impact to impart the loft required to achieve the 'floating' trajectory.

Have you ever noticed that whenever you mishit the ball towards a bunker it always seems to have just enough strength to trickle in? Whether that's great thinking on the course designer's behalf or just bad luck on yours, it leaves you facing this little beauty, where the ball has come to rest almost against the back

WORKING WITH A
RESTRICTED
BACKSWING

lip. It's a nasty proposition, even for the most accomplished of bunker players.

Because the priority here is avoiding the back lip of the bunker, it goes without saying that your backswing is going to be fairly wristy. In fact, it's all wrists – there's no real arm swing or shoulder turn.

To facilitate an early wrist hinge, I set up with virtually all my weight on my left side, where it remains throughout the shot. I also choke down on the grip to shorten the shaft and I sometimes open the face a little to get at least some control over the ball, which invariably shoots off low and fast. Finally, I rehearse my takeaway a few times until I'm confident of being able to comfortably clearing the lip.

There's not much finesse involved here. Basically, it's just a straight chop up and down with the wrists. I concentrate on keeping my body as 'quiet' as possible, since the slightest weight shift onto my right side could be enough to send the club straight into the lip.

Setting up with the majority of your weight on your left side and keeping it there throughout the shot will give you the feeling of being able to hinge your wrists up and down sharply without shifting your weight across onto your right side.

Because the ball will always shoot off low and fast from this type of lie, I'll often open up the clubface a little to try and get some extra height and, therefore, control on the shot.

"Don't set your sights too high with this shot. Instead, be satisfied with simply getting the ball onto the green and rolling first time. Knocking it stiff from this kind of lie requires perfect technique, lots of experience and more than your fair share of luck"

There's no need to panic when you find your ball lying on a tricky upslope or downslope in a bunker. Once you understand the adjustments you need to make to your address position, you'll soon be able to play these shots comfortably and confidently.

From an uphill sloping lie in a bunker the ball will always fly high and land softly. The cardinal sin here is obviously leaving the ball well short of the pin, so don't be afraid to be aggressive through impact. Hit hard.

PLAYING FROM AN
UPSLOPE

The key to playing from any kind of sloping lie, uphill or downhill, is to set your body perpendicular to the slope. This has the effect of recreating a flat lie by aligning your shoulders parallel to the ground, enabling you to make an approximation to your normal swing without too many adjustments.

As you can see here, I've tilted my spine backwards so that my shoulders and hips are now square to the ground, which has forced my weight onto my back foot. This address position, combined with the launching pad effect of the uphill slope, will produce a high, floaty type of shot which will virtually stop dead on landing, rolling only 12 to 18 inches at most.

The obvious danger here is dropping the ball well short of the pin, so to ensure that I carry the ball far enough through the air, I'll often play this shot with the face of my sand wedge square instead of open. Once I've made these adjustments, I simply go ahead and make my normal swing, concentrating on hitting really hard through impact to generate enough force to carry the ball all the way to the hole.

The address position is critical. Set your shoulders perpendicular to the downslope and allow your weight to fall naturally onto your left foot. Now you can go ahead and make your normal swing, safe in the knowledge that you'll be swinging with the slope rather than fighting against it.

NEGOTIATING A DOWN SLOPE

Although playing from a downslope in the sand is arguably far more difficult than from an uphill lie, the principle of setting your spine at right angles to the slope remains the same. This time, however, you should tilt your spine forwards slightly to square up your shoulders and hips to the slope, naturally nudging your weight onto your left foot.

It's always difficult to predict exactly how the ball will fly from this type of lie but one thing is certain, it will always shoot off low and fast with plenty of topspin, so you may encounter difficulties stopping the ball short of the hole. To counteract the extended roll, I usually choke down on the grip and play these shots with the face slightly open, which gives me a little extra height on the shot and therefore more control of the ball and a soft landing.

Another key to playing this shot well is to maintain your rhythm. Whenever there is an element of doubt or hesitancy in your mind over your ability to play a shot, you will find a tendency to swing too fast to get the shot over and done with. But, as this sequence shows, I've consciously kept my tempo smooth and unhurried all the way through to a balanced, relaxed and very comfortable finish position.

Contrary to what you may have thought, playing this shot isn't just a case of hit and hope. If you make the right adjustments at address and swing through rhythmically into a relaxed and comfortable finish position like this, you stand a great chance of escaping unscathed.

Try not to be intimidated by an awkward lie like this in a bunker. Always take the time to assess the situation and then approach the shot with a positive frame of mind.

"Whenever the ball is below the level of your feet, the heel of the club will always make contact with the sand first and the ball will fly to the right. Counteract this by closing the face of your sand wedge"

CLOSE THE
FACE

When the ball is below your feet

How many of you fancy your chances of getting up and down in two from this position? I don't either, but here goes. You can play this shot two ways, as I am here, bending over sharply from the waist to reach the ball, or off your knees if the ball is a long way below your feet. Whichever method you choose, however, you'll need to make a few adjustments to compensate for the slope and the awkward lie of the ball.

Your first priority is to achieve comfort and balance at address. Flex your knees and tilt from the waist to bring your body and the clubhead down to the level of the ball. To maximise the length

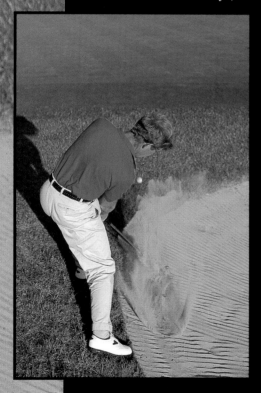

Nobody likes playing these types of shots, but if you make the right adjustments at address to bring yourself down to the level of the ball, and furnish your technique with a smooth rhythm, there's no reason whatsoever why you shouldn't be able to escape from this tricky lie first time and get the ball fairly close to the flag.

of the club, hold it right at the end of the grip and place the ball in the middle of your stance. Finally, make two or three practice swings to ensure that you can play the shot without toppling head first straight into the trap.

Whenever the ball is below the level of your feet on a slope like this, the heel of the club will always make contact with the sand first, where it will either dig in or bounce off the slope resulting in plenty of fat or shanked shots. To counteract this, I always play this shot with a closed clubface. This serves two purposes: firstly, it moves the heel back and ensures that the whole of the clubface makes contact with the sand at the same time; secondly, physics dictate that the ball will always shoot off sharply to the right from this kind of slope, but hooding the face will nullify this effect.

Accepting that the lie of the ball and the angle of your spine will combine to steepen the plane of your backswing, simply treat the shot just like any other from the sand. Focus on maintaining good rhythm, particularly as you start your down-

swing, and remember to accelerate the club smoothly and confidently through impact.

THE LONG
RANGE
BUNKER SHOT

I'm sure you don't need me to tell you that bunker shots increase in difficulty the farther away you are from the green. I know that the maximum distance I can hit the ball by swinging flat out using my basic splash technique with a sand wedge is just under 30 yards. For anything over that range, I have to find other ways of generating more power.

Up to about 50 yards or so from the green you have a couple of options to choose from: assuming that you don't have too much of a raised lip to negotiate, you can either stay with your sand wedge to play the shot, but square up your

To increase the distance you can hit the ball from the sand, square up your stance, play the ball towards the centre of your feet and don't be afraid to make a full backswing.

106

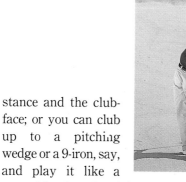

Because the extra spin imparted by taking only a tiny amount of sand with the shot will stop the ball quickly once it hits the green, you can afford to be aggressive through impact and fly the ball all the way to the pin.

stance and the club-face; or you can club up to a pitching wedge or a 9-iron, say, and play it like a normal bunker shot. Nine times out of ten I'll take the second option.

Here, though, I'm about 65 yards from the green and can't reach it using my normal splash technique. I've therefore chosen a pitching wedge to play the shot and, to help make the distance, I square up my stance, play the ball more towards the middle of my feet and aim to take less sand with the shot, just half an inch or so instead of the normal inch.

Obviously, precision is crucial here, so one of my key thoughts is to retain a smooth tempo and keep my body fairly 'quiet'. A fraction too much sand can be the difference between reaching the green and coming up 10 yards short.

It's also worth noting that you still have to be fairly aggressive with the shot, while at the same time remaining in full control. If you concentrate on accelerating the club smoothly through impact into a well-balanced and comfortable finish you should have no trouble in getting the ball up to the hole.

"When you're playing a long range bunker shot, keep your rhythm smooth and your body as 'quiet' as possible. A fraction too much sand with the shot can be the difference between reaching the green and coming up well short"

If you're struggling to play good bunker shots, it's more than likely that a faulty address position is to blame for your problems.
Make sure that your feet hips and shoulders all aim well left of the target, but that the face of your sand wedge aims directly at the pin.
From here, all you need to do is swing back along the line of your feet and you'll automatically cut across the ball at impact.

TONY'S TIP

Learn to swing along the right lines

Swinging across the ball-to-target line from an open address position is one of the key fundamentals for playing consistent bunker shots. The next time you work on your bunker play, draw a couple of lines in the sand as I've done here (right) to remind yourself of the correct swing path.

As I mentioned at the start of this section bunker shots should nearly always be played with an open stance, your feet, hips and shoulders aiming well left of the target. From this position you simply swing back along the line of your feet and shoulders to play the shot. In other words, you swing across the target line.

If you're having trouble getting to grips with this method and still feel as though you want to swing the club inside, try this exercise. Draw a couple of lines in the sand, one along the line of your feet so that it points left of the target, the other parallel to the first to illustrate your swing path.

As you take the club away, make sure you swing the clubhead along the line you've drawn in the sand. This may feel strange to start with, particularly if you're used to swinging the club well inside the line on the way back, but it will produce a much better angle of attack and therefore more consistent results.

One last point – this is a practice drill only. Don't be tempted to draw lines in the sand when you find yourself facing a bunker shot in your monthly medal, unless, of course, you find the idea of a two-shot penalty appealing!

TONY'S
TIP

The length and speed of your swing controls distance from sand

Many players believe that to vary the distance you hit the ball from the sand, you should either increase or decrease the distance you hit behind the ball. In other words, you should take a lot of sand if you want to move the ball just a few yards and only a little if you want to hit a longer shot.

That's far too complicated for me. My own method is much simpler: I aim to take the same amount of sand on each and every shot and simply control the distance I hit the ball by altering the length of my backswing and the force with which I hit the ball.

If I want to play a shot of around 10 yards, say, I'll make a three-quarter length swing then hit through fairly gently. On longer shots I'll make almost a full swing and hit down much harder. Exactly how far I take the club back and how hard I hit is something which comes with experience but, if you spend some time experimenting from the sand, you'll soon develop a feel for how to play the shot.

5. put

ting

Putting has often been described as a game within a game and, all things considered, that's a fairly accurate description. While nailing the ball 270 yards down the middle of the fairway off the tee requires a combination of hand-to-eye co-ordination, timing and physical strength, 'stroking' in a tricky little four or five-footer , a task which on the surface appears

THE GAME
WITHIN
THE GAME

simple in comparison, tests your mental resolve to its maximum and is equally demanding in its own way, some might say more so.

Without exception, all of the world's top golfers can hit the ball long and straight off the tee, all of them can hit their irons crisply and accurately, and all of them are good putters. But that's not enough these days: to win tournaments at the very top level of the game, and particularly major championships, you have to be a great putter, and that means spending many hours on the practice green.

You only have to spend some time watching the pros at a tournament to see how seriously they take this part of their game and how many hours they devote to their quest for putting perfection. It's not uncommon to see players working on their stroke until it gets so dark they can no longer see the ball, let alone the hole, and even then the caddie literally has to drag them away from the course.

While I don't expect you to spend anywhere near this amount of time 'grooving' your own putting stroke, I will point out that putting accounts for around 40 per cent of the shots played in a round of golf and that the amount of time you spend working on your putting in your practice sessions should reflect this. The rewards will be well worth it in the long run because a good putter is a match for anyone.

"Putting accounts for around **40** per cent of the shots played in a round of golf. It therefore makes sense to spend **40** per cent of your practice time on this important area of the game. You only have to watch the top pros at a tournament to see how much time they devote to enhancing their putting skills. If yo do the same, you'll be a match for anyone"

MY PUTTING STROKE

Comfort breeds confidence at address

You only have to look at the wide variety of putting styles on Tour to realise that there are no set rules when it comes to putting. Jack Nicklaus, for example, crouches low over the ball with an open stance, while Greg Norman stands very upright and closed. Fred Couples putts with his left hand below right on the club, Ben Crenshaw grips the club conventionally right hand below left, while Bernhard Langer separates his hands on the grip completely. Mike Hulbert, an American player on the USPGA Tour, even putts one-handed!

But despite their obvious differences, these players have one thing in common – they all look relaxed and comfortable over the ball. I believe that comfort breeds confidence. If you are comfortable, you really feel as though you can make a smooth, uninhibited stroke. But if you feel cramped, unbalanced and generally out of sorts at address, this is nearly always reflected in an awkward and tentative jab at the ball.

Pay particular attention to your posture. As I've already said, there are no set rules, but I do believe it's a good idea to try and set up with your eyes directly over the ball as this will give you a more accurate perspective on the line of the putt. Also, allow your arms to hang down fairly naturally, with just a slight bend at the elbows to ensure they are free from tension. From this relaxed and comfortable set-up position, I can move the putter away smoothly and accelerate it confidently towards the hole.

The stroke – a combination of hands, arms and shoulders

I don't believe in having too many putting thoughts. In my opinion, good putting is 90 percent confidence and inspiration and only 10 percent technique. But, having said that, confidence emanates from having a reliable stroke that you believe in. Once I've set up over the ball, I like to free my mind completely from complicated theory and just let things take their natural course.

However, I do believe it's a good idea to have one simple thought on which to focus, and mine is maintaining the "Y" formed between my arms and the shaft of the putter throughout the stroke. This ensures that my shoulders, arms and hands combine to move the putter away from the ball, which keeps my wrists firm and my rhythm smooth. Some coaches are of the opinion that controlling the putting stroke with a pendulum-style rocking of the shoulders is a more reliable method but, while I agree that too much emphasis on 'hands' in the stroke can be dangerous, I find that eliminating them completely restricts your feel and hinders your ability to judge the pace of the putt.

Accelerate the putter smoothly towards the hole

Once I've moved the putter away from the ball, all I really think about in the through-swing is accelerating the putter confidently towards the hole, again ensuring that the "Y" formed at address remains intact and that my rhythm remains smooth. I've no conscious thought of trying to hit at the ball; I simply let it get in the way of the swinging motion of the putter.

Accelerating the clubhead really does form the foundation of a solid stroke. A firmly struck putt will not only have more chance of reaching the hole, but is also less likely to be affected by inconsistencies on the green, such as spike marks, debris and footprints, and will also hold its line better.

Having said that, I'm the first to admit how difficult it is to force yourself to do it, particularly when the greens are slick. For example, when I first played in the Masters in 1993, the pace of the Augusta National greens, combined with the severe undulations, made them frighteningly quick and intimidating. I found it difficult not to putt defensively, but I had to convince myself that the only way I was going to hole anything at all was to be assertive and trust myself to accelerate the putter head.

Let me also draw your attention to two points. Firstly, look at how firm my hands are throughout the stroke. From address, through impact and into the followthrough, there's no breakdown, no 'flicking' at the ball. Secondly, see how my head has stayed down until well after the ball has left the putter face. This keeps your body 'quiet' during the stroke and your shoulders square to the line, which ensures that the putter will travel along the correct path.

MY PUTTING STROKE

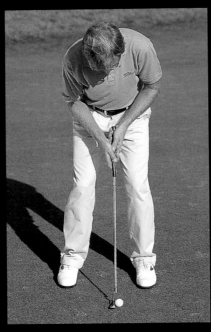

*Comfort is the key at address. Let your arms
hang naturally with a slight bend at the elbows.
Set up with your eyes directly over the ball.*

*Your hands, arms and shoulders work together
to move the putter away from the ball.
Make sure that you maintain the "Y".*

*Accelerate the putter smoothly through to the
hole. Keep your wrists firm, head down and
resist the temptation to hit at the ball.*

*Lead the putter through to the target with the
back of your left hand. Stay down until the ball
has left the face and is rolling towards the hole.*

MY PUTTING GRIP

The reverse overlap

Just as there is no single particular putting style suitable for everybody, so there is no particular putting grip which is universally ideal either. My own opinion is that if your grip feels comfortable and it enables you to hole a lot of putts, then whatever you do, don't change it. Enjoy it while it lasts!

If you're not quite so happy, however, I recommend that you try the reverse overlap grip, which I and the majority of players on Tour use nowadays. To form this grip, take hold of the club with your left hand as you would normally, but extend your index finger down the shaft. Now apply your right hand and let your left index finger rest on top of the last three fingers of your right hand. The little finger on your right hand can either rest tightly against the second finger of your left hand or it can rest lightly on top of it, depending on what feels comfortable to you.

I find that this grip, where my palms face each other in a neutral position, gives me the sensation of my hands working together as a single unit throughout the stroke, heightening my sense of feel and giving me confidence to accelerate the putter towards the hole without the fear of one hand becoming too dominant.

As to grip pressure, it should be light enough to enable you to 'feel' the pace of the putt, but not quite so loose that the putter can actually twist in your hands as you make your stroke. As a general rule, the correct grip pressure is firm enough for you to hold the club securely, but without any noticeable tension or tightness in your hands or forearms.

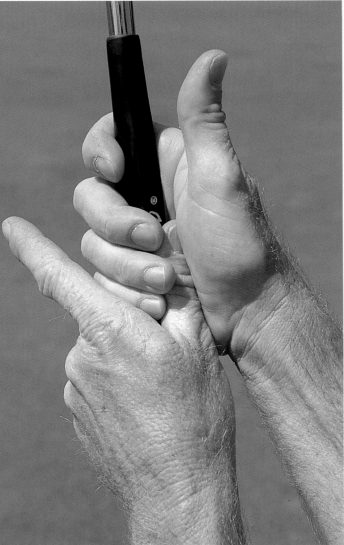

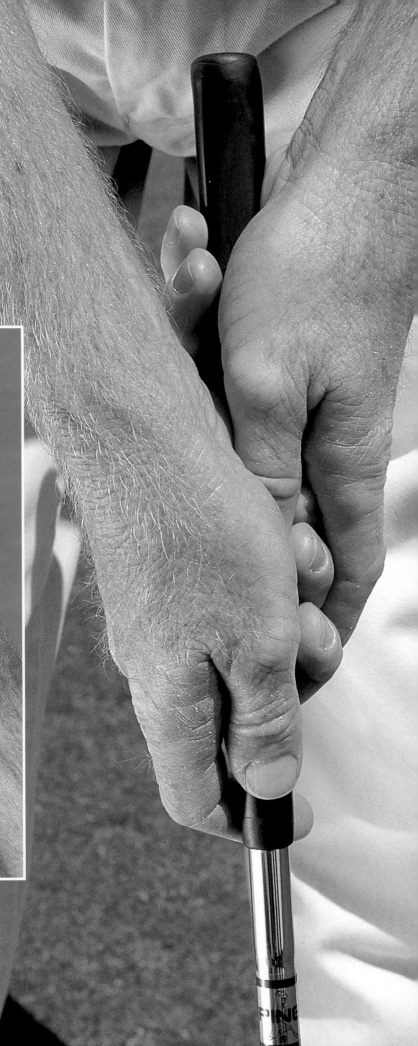

The reverse overlap grip illustrated here is favoured by the majority of Tour professionals these days as it keeps the hands and wrists firm throughout the putting stroke.

PUTTING STYLES

A purely personal affair

While most players these days tend to be fairly orthodox in their technique and approach to the long game, when it comes to putting you can throw the text book right out of the window. Putting is, and always will be, a purely personal affair. For example, Gary Player has a very 'handsy' stroke and likes to jab the ball into the hole with his wrists. Nick Faldo, on the other hand, prefers to control the stroke with a pendulum-style rocking of his shoulders while

"Two of the game's best ever putters, Jack Nicklaus and Bernhard Langer, wouldn't score many points for artistic impression on the greens, but they would get perfect sixes every time for technical merit"

124

"Looks aren't important when it comes to putting. Only the end result matters. I've often said that if standing on my head and holding my putter between my knees would help me hole more putts, I would do it without a second thought"

When it comes to putting technique you can throw the text book right out of the window. Obviously, there are fundamentals, but there are no set rules, no rights or wrongs – all that matters is whether your own method enables you to hole a lot of putts.

Only through practice, experimentation and a great deal of trial and error will you find a putting method which suits you personally. One of the unique things about golf is that there are just as many putting styles as there are players.

his hands remain relatively passive. Both players have holed many a crunch putt in their time, so who's to say which technique is correct?

Only through practice, experimentation and a great deal of trial and error will you find a putting method that suits you personally. Don't worry about what it looks like, either. I've always said that if standing on my head and holding the putter between my knees would help me hole more putts, I would do it without a second thought. Jack Nicklaus and Bernhard Langer wouldn't win any prizes for artistic impression on the greens, but they would get perfect sixes every time for technical merit.

FOR SOLID WRISTS, TRY PUTTING
CACK-HANDED

Putting with the left hand below the right on the grip, often referred to as 'cack-handed', is now a common sight on Tour, with Nick Faldo and Fred Couples among some of the players who have swapped their conventional putting style for this new variation.

As I've already mentioned, one of the keys to consistent putting is to keep the wrists firm. If they break down or collapse through impact, the hands work independently from the arms and shoulders and the putter face develops a mind of its own, which invariably means big trouble. Placing the left hand below the right helps many players achieve a feeling of solidity in their wrists and also gives them the sensation of being able to lead the putter head through to the target with the back of their left hand, thus ensuring a smooth, confident acceleration.

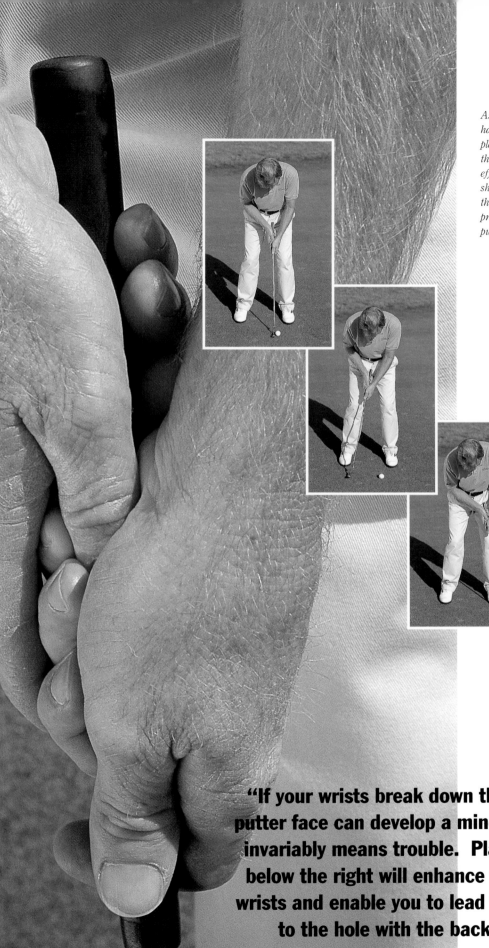

As well as keeping your hands out of the stroke, placing your left hand below the right on the grip has the effect of levelling up your shoulders at address, therefore making it easier to produce a pendulum-style putting stroke.

"If your wrists break down through impact, the putter face can develop a mind of its own, which invariably means trouble. Placing the left hand below the right will enhance the solidity in your wrists and enable you to lead the putter through to the hole with the back of your left hand"

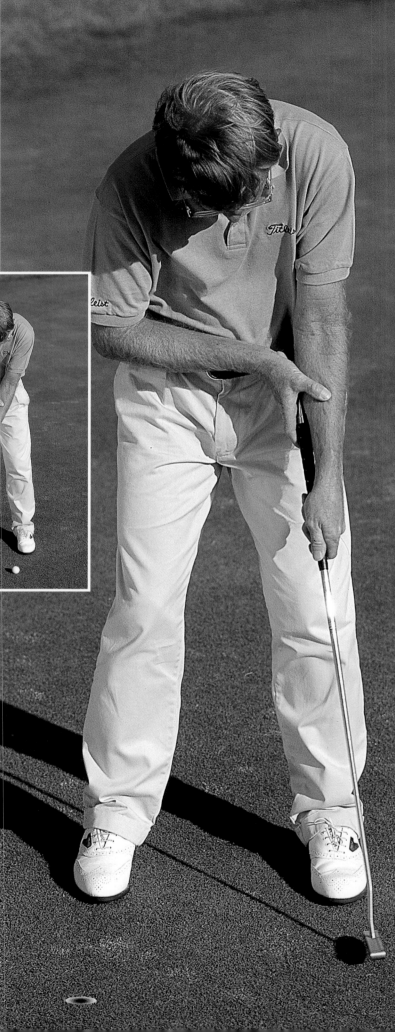

The Langer grip can help eradicate the 'yips' as it keeps the hands well apart on the club, making it impossible for the wrists to break down through impact or for one hand to dominate the stroke.

"Most players who have managed to successfully overcome the putting 'yips' have done so by separating their hands on the club"

BEAT THE
YIPS

With the Langer grip

Once the hands and arms are locked in place on the grip, the putting stroke is controlled entirely by the shoulders. Simply rock them up and down in a pendulum-style fashion to move the putter back and through towards the hole.

Like most of my colleagues on Tour, I'm full of admiration for Bernhard Langer, not simply because he has managed to successfully overcome several bouts of putting 'yips' during his career (an amazing feat in itself), but also because he has shown immense mental strength and character in erasing any trace of those negative thoughts from his mind to become one of the very best putters in the world of golf today.

Many youngsters reading this book will have no idea of how painful it sometimes was to watch Bernhard putting – it really was a sorry sight. However, as we all know, it's a totally different story today. If I had to nominate any player in the world to putt for my life, Bernhard would be right there at the very top of my short list.

The 'yips' is a term used to describe a general inability to control the putter, particularly on short putts where the pressure is at its greatest. The yips can manifest themselves as either an involuntary snatch at the ball in the putting stroke, a nervy, tentative prod or,

most commonly, a breaking down of the wrists at impact. Whichever way, the problem is predominantly a mental one.

Most players like Langer who have successfully beaten the 'yips' have done so by separating their hands on the club. As I'm demonstrating here, Langer's grip is an extension of the 'cack-hand' grip theory illustrated on the previous page. Bernhard places his left hand well down the grip and positions the shaft so that it lays against his left forearm. His next step is to clasp the fingers of his right hand around his left forearm, holding the shaft of the putter firmly in place as he does so.

If you're sitting in your living room as you read this, with a putter in your hands experimenting with this grip, try now hingeing your wrists. You should find that you can't. They're both locked firmly in place – and that's the whole idea. Once he sets up over the ball, Bernhard simply rocks his shoulders up and down in a pendulum-style fashion to swing the putter back and through to the hole without any outside interference at all from the hands.

Without doubt, it's an extremely solid and efficient putting stroke and one which you would do well to try if your own short-range putting isn't quite as good as it should be.

Love them or hate them, broomhandle putters are here to stay. Sam Torrance certainly prompted a few raised eyebrows when he unveiled his specially extended putter back in the 80s, but since then many of the game's top players have gone on to achieve considerable worldwide success after switching to this controversial method of putting.

The theory behind the broomhandle putter is that if you place the end of the putter shaft firmly against your chin or chest and keep it there throughout the stroke, you create a pendulum effect, meaning that, once you set

THE BROOMHANDLE

METHOD

Creating the perfect pendulum effect

the putter in motion, it will automatically travel back to the ball along the correct path.

Regardless of whether you prefer the chin or chest method, grip the end of the putter lightly between the thumb and index finger of your left hand to hold the putter in place and form the axis to your stroke. From here, move the putter away smoothly with your right hand and then just allow gravity and momentum to do the rest. Obviously, don't let go of the putter completely, just guide it back to the ball along the line it naturally wants to travel on, and into your follow-through.

Needless to say, you must keep your head and upper body very steady with this putting method. If your head or chest moves about all over the place, you ruin the pendulum effect.

"Regardless of whether you opt for the 'chin' or the more popular 'chest' method, the key is to keep your axis point stationary and your grip pressure light.

Otherwise you'll destroy the pendulum effect and with it your chances of making a smooth, sweeping stroke"

Once you set the putter moving, keep your grip pressure light and allow your right hand to simply guide the putter head back and through to the hole.

HOW TO READ
GREENS

The ability to read greens evolves through years and years experience of playing golf on a wide variety of courses in different countries and climates throughout the world. Many of the intricacies, and indeed vagaries, involved cannot therefore be satisfactorily explained within the pages of a book. For example, how do you explain being able to look at what appears to be a left-to-right breaking putt, yet knowing that the ball is going to move up the hill because of the severity of the grain? How can the hole look as big as a bucket one day and the size of a thimble the next? Why is it that on some days you can walk onto every green, immediately spot the line, acclimatise to the pace and hole just about everything in sight, yet the very next day, on the very same course even, you can't buy yourself a putt?

What I'm trying to say is that reading greens is, for the most part, inspirational, not mechanical. Having said that, there are also many identifiable factors which you can use to help determine the way in which a ball will behave on the green. Over the next few pages, I'll be passing on almost 30 years of green-reading experience.

132

MY GREEN READING
ROUTINE

If you start looking for the break on a putt only when you actually get to your ball on the green, you're missing out on a whole wealth of valuable information. I start reading a green as soon as I have played my approach shot and am within about 30 yards of the putting surface. From this distance, I find I can get a better perspective of the overall lie of the land and that slopes are far more easily identifiable than they are when you're standing right on top of them.

While I'm making my way towards the green, I'm consciously (and probably subconsciously) absorbing all kinds of subtle information that will help me determine how the ball will roll. The speed and direction of the wind, for example, how firm the ground is underfoot, perhaps, or just simply the slope in relation to buildings, trees or telephone poles in the background. All of this helps me to decide which way I think the ball will break or react.

Once I reach my ball, I view the putt from three angles. Starting from behind the ball, I

Sweden's Joakim Haegmann is renowned for his worm's eye view inspection of greens. I don't quite go that far, but I do try to get down as low as possible to see the break.

crouch down as low as I can to ground level to ensure that I see every possible contour. Then I take a look from behind the hole, either to confirm my initial assessment or, if I'm still undecided after my first look, to form a clearer picture in my mind of which way I believe the

ball will move. I also make a point of carefully inspecting the grass around the edge of the hole, as it's here that the ball will break most when it begins to run out of steam.

Finally, I take a look at the putt from side on to see whether it is predominantly uphill, downhill, or perhaps a combination of the two. This last look is vitally important and should never be ignored, as it will confirm the pace of the putt, which should always be your prime consideration. It's impossible to establish the line of a putt without first assessing its speed.

THE SPEED INFLUENCING FACTORS

Once I've determined how the natural contours of the green will affect the putt, I start to look for elements which will either increase or decrease the break. I believe there are four factors which can affect the speed and, therefore, the line of a putt: 1) wind; 2) gradient; 3) conditions (wet or dry); 4) grain. Let's look at each of these factors in a little more detail.

1. Wind

As anyone who has hit one of their best drives into a fierce headwind and watched in absolute horror as the ball has ballooned up into the air and come back to fall almost at his feet will tell you, the wind can have a major effect on your shots. There's no doubting the fact that the higher you hit the ball the more it will be at the mercy of the wind, but that doesn't necessarily mean your ball is safe when it's on the green.

Although a mild breeze is unlikely to knock a well-struck putt too far off line, a strong, howling wind can move the ball by up to a couple of inches. At the Open Championship at St Andrews in 1995, for example, I had a dead straight three-footer on the 12th hole, which missed the hole by a good six inches and then went on to move another four feet to the right. So, always remember to allow for a little extra movement on the putt when there's a strong sidewind blowing and either hit the ball harder or slightly softer, depending on whether you're putting with the wind or against it.

> **"Always allow for a little extra movement on the putt when there's a significant sidewind blowing"**

2. Gradient

You won't need me to tell you that you have to hit the ball harder on an uphill putt than you do on a downhill one – that's common sense, but there's more to it than that. The severity of the slope will also determine the break. How many times have you faced a tricky downhiller, tried to 'die' the ball into the hole and watched in utter disbelief as the ball trickled away from the cup right at the last minute? A few, I'll bet.

A slow-moving putt will always move considerably more than a fast moving one, which is why I always play less break on an uphill putt, where I have to give the ball a good rap, and more break on a downhiller where less force is required to get the ball to the hole.

4. Grain

On most golf courses throughout Europe and the United States, the grass on the greens is of a very fine bent or fescue variety. Because this species of grass can be cut very short, it never gets a chance to grow in any one particular direction, and doesn't really influence either the pace or line of the putt.

If you travel down to South Africa or indeed to any country with a very hot climate, however, you'll find that the grass is much coarser. Because of this, the blades are longer and tend to lay flat and grow in one direction, often towards water or the sun. This is called 'grain' and it can have a major effect on both the speed and line of your putts.

The most difficult thing about putting on grainy greens is judging pace. Down grain, a putt can be as quick as lightning, but coming back it can often be like putting into glue. Equally, if you're facing a left-to-righter and the grain is growing in sympathy, you need to allow for even more movement. I've even known grain to move the ball up a slope.

A good way of identifying the direction of the grain is to inspect the hole. If the grain is left to right, say, expect to see signs of wear on the right edge of the cup, as most of the putts will be dropping on this side and the greenkeeper's mower will pull out some of the grass instead of cutting it cleanly. Another method is to see if your spikes catch when you walk. If they do, you can safely assume that you're putting straight into the grain. The biggest giveaway, however, is the texture of the grass. Down grain, the grass will look shiny and glossy; into the grain, it will look dull and much darker.

Left: Charting greens plays an important role in my pre-tournament preparation.
Above: By providing a vertical reference point, plumb bobbing is a popular way of spotting the break on a putt.

3. Conditions

Another contributing factor which significantly affects the pace and break of a putt is the condition of the green. Just like a downhill putt, the ball will always break more on a fast, dry surface because less force is needed to get the ball to the hole and the ball has more time to turn. Wet greens, on the other hand, have the complete opposite effect. Water slows the pace of the green and causes friction between the ball and the grass, thereby forcing you to hit the putt more firmly.

> **"A putt will break more when the green is fast and dry than it will when the surface is slow and wet"**

TONY'S TIP

Treat every putt as straight

In my experience, amateur golfers are generally fairly good at reading the slopes on greens, but they struggle to commit themselves to the line of the putt. Quite often I see them trying to steer the ball towards the hole in an effort to hold it up against a slope. That's a three-putt method if ever I saw one.

A great piece of putting advice I was given as a youngster was to treat every putt as straight. This may sound strange to you, but it's really quite logical. Once you've studied the putt and have reached the conclusion that it's going to break six inches from the left, say, you can forget about the hole completely. Simply align your putter six inches to the left of the hole and set up with your feet, hips and shoulders square to that line. Now all you have to do is go ahead and make your normal stroke, set the ball rolling six inches to the left of the hole and let gravity do the rest. Sounds easy, doesn't it? And it is.

TONY'S TIP

Use buildings to help you read slopes

I have always been a notoriously bad reader of slope, which is why I've learnt so many tricks to make this facet of putting a little easier. I've always been careful to employ caddies with good eyesight. When I see a putt as moving a couple of inches from the left, say, but my caddie says it moves slightly from the right, often I'll go with his read. One of the reasons I love putting on a course where there are plenty of buildings around is that roof tops and walls make perfect horizontal and vertical reference points against which I can determine the overall lie of the green. The same holds true for water and trees, which respectively lie flat and grow vertically, as they enable you to detect any slight variation at all from the perpendicular.

Here, using the roof of the small building behind the green as a reference, I can tell immediately that the green slopes considerably from right to left and can therefore allow for the break accordingly.

If you consistently struggle to get the ball up to the hole, chances are you're decelerating the putter through impact. To ensure that you accelerate the putter through confidently towards the hole, reduce the length of your backswing and increase the length of your followthrough.

LEAVING PUTTS
SHORT?

Make a shorter backswing and a longer follow-through

'Never up, never in' may have become something of a golfing cliché over the years, but the message is still valid. If you don't get the ball to the hole, it won't drop – simple as that. All of us are guilty of leaving putts short every now and then, but for most amateurs it's an all too frequent and frustrating occurrence.

In my experience, golfers who consistently struggle to get the ball to the hole take the putter back too far and then decelerate through impact. If that sounds familiar, this exercise will help you groove a more purposeful putting stroke. To curtail the length of your backswing, place a tee peg in the ground a few inches

behind the ball. Now go ahead and make your normal putting stroke, but do not touch the peg as you move the putter away. By reducing the length of your backswing, this exercise automatically forces you to accelerate the putter through to the hole. Try it and see how compact and authoritative your putting stroke becomes.

TONY'S
TIP

*Aim the putter first,
then your body*

Everybody knows the importance of good alignment, but most golfers assume that it's a fundamental which applies only to the long game – they couldn't be more wrong. When hitting a driver off the tee, you can have a margin for error of anywhere between 20 and 40 yards, or more. When you're facing a putt, however, that margin for error is reduced to just a couple of inches, the width of the cup.

I recommend that you make good alignment an integral part of your putting routine. The best way of lining up correctly to the hole is to start by aiming the face of the putter at your intended target with your right hand. Once you are happy that the club is aiming where you want it, step into the shot and then build your stance around the face of the putter. Do it the other way round and I guarantee that your alignment will be way out each and every time.

Because the target is that much smaller, good alignment in putting is just as important as it is in the long game, if not more so. Through years of experience I've found that the best way of lining up correctly to the hole is to start by aiming the face of the putter at the intended target with my right hand. Once I'm happy that the club is aiming where I want it, I step into the shot and build my stance around the face of the putter. That way, my body alignment complements my putter face alignment, which gives me the confidence to make a smooth, positive stroke.

Whether you prefer to stand slightly closed or open to a putt isn't too important. What's vital is that you aim the putter at the hole before you form your address position. If you try to manipulate the putter face into position once you've set up, your body will be aiming one way and your putter another. Not surprisingly, you'll stand little chance of holing the putt.

LOOKING UP FAR
TOO EARLY?

Follow Nick Faldo's example and wait for the ball to drop

Nobody likes those awkward putts of four or five feet, particularly if they come with the added pressure of having to make them to save par or to avoid losing the hole. In view of this, most short putts are missed simply because players get nervous and look up too early to see where the ball has gone, often before the putter makes contact with the ball. I know, because I'm guilty of it myself at times.

Lifting your head up to look at the hole has a knock-on effect to your shoulders, causing them to spin out to the left. When this happens, the putt can go literally anywhere, but it will usually miss on the left side.

On putts of this length, I try to discipline myself to stay down until the ball is well on its way to the hole. Often I'll pick out a blade of grass just a fraction behind the ball and focus on that until the ball is rolling. Of course, it is difficult and how well I actually manage it depends on the importance of the putt and how twitchy I'm feeling at the time. Nick Faldo is particularly disciplined at doing this. Whether he's standing over a two-footer or a 52-footer, he stays down until he hears the ball rattle into the back of the hole or until it has obviously missed.

To prevent yourself from looking up too early to find out whether or not you have missed the putt, pick out a blade of grass behind the ball and stay focussed on that spot as you make your stroke and until you hear the ball rattle into the back of the hole.

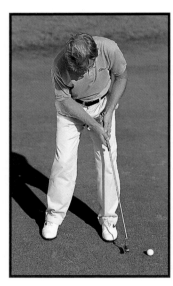

TRAP THE BALL FOR
SOLID WRISTS

As I mentioned earlier in this section over-active hands in the putting stroke can often be a recipe for disaster. A good way of checking to see whether or not your stroke is too wristy is to trap a ball between your left forearm and the inside of the putting grip, then go ahead and make your normal putting stroke. You may find this drill more effective if you choke down by a couple of inches on the grip.

"If your hands and wrists tend to break down through impact, this practice drill will help keep them out of the stroke"

If you start to 'flick' at the ball with your right hand, or if your wrists show any signs of breaking down through impact, the butt end of the grip will move backwards and the ball will fall to the floor. If this happens, bend down, pick it up and repeat the drill until your hands and wrists are solid enough through impact to keep the ball in place throughout your stroke.

To appreciate the
relationship between
your hands, arms and
shoulders in the
putting stroke,
practise your putting
with a shaft trapped
between your arms
and chest.
Ensure that the 'Y'
formed between your
forearms and the
putter remains intact
throughout.

STAY CONNECTED FOR A CONSISTENT
STROKE

Here's a great exercise for 'grooving' the sensation of your hands, arms and shoulders working together to produce a repetitive putting stroke. Trap the shaft of a club between your arms and chest, address the ball and hit a few practice putts, ensuring that the shaft stays in place as you make your stroke. If you perform this drill correctly, you should find that it becomes impossible for your hands to move independently from your arms and shoulders. Work specifically on the feeling of your hands, arms and upper body working as a synchronised unit, and on furnishing the stroke with a fluid rhythm. If you can devote just a few minutes each day working on this drill, your putting will improve dramatically.

To improve my awareness of the role both hands actually play in the putting stroke, I'll often spend time on the practice putting green stroking balls into the hole with just one hand.

Because it really forces you to concentrate on what you are doing, putting one-handed is an excellent way of restoring lost rhythm control and feel. It also magnifies any little flaws you may have in your stroke.

ONE-HANDED
FOR FEEL AND CONTROL

I've often boasted that I'm the best one-handed putter in the world – really! I can step onto any practice putting green, stand up to a putt and lay the ball stone dead to the hole almost every time from long range using just one hand. Although I'm sure I would lack the courage of my convictions if it actually came to the crunch, it sometimes makes me wonder why I don't putt like that in tournaments!

Seriously, though, putting with either hand is a great way of improving your rhythm and feel and generally increasing your awareness of the role both hands play in the stroke. Putting with just your right hand helps you to concentrate on maintaining the angle at the back of your right wrist, thereby promoting a feeling of solidity, while putting with just your left hand forces you to work on the feeling of guiding and accelerating the putter through towards the hole with the back of the left wrist and forearm, and of the club staying square to the line of the putt well into your follow-through.

Combine those two elements and you have the makings of a great putting stroke.

KEEP YOUR STROKE ON THE
STRAIGHT
AND NARROW

P hysics dictates that as your stroke increases in length the putter will naturally move inside the line on the way back. From close range, however, it's preferable for the putter to move back and through on a straight line. Try this drill to groove the feeling of a square-to-square putting stroke.

Lay down a couple of shafts on the green like this, parallel to the hole and just over a putter-width apart. Next, place a ball between the two shafts and aim your putter directly at the hole. Now go ahead and make a few practice putts, ensuring that the putter stays between the two shafts as it swings straight back and through. As long as you have lined up the shafts correctly, you'll find that you just can't miss.

If you spend just ten minutes or so working on this exercise before you head for the first tee, I guarantee that you'll be absolutely amazed at your ability to hole out with confidence.

"On short putts I believe that if you aim at the centre of the cup and strike the ball firmly you'll hole out almost every time. Sure, you'll miss the odd one, but it'll be the exception"

154

PRACTISE THE TOUGH PUTTS

Plenty of golfers ask me what the secret is to holing those testing, little three- or four-footers. Well, the answer is simple – aggression and confidence. Over the years, I've found that when I try to 'nurse' the ball into the hole from just a few feet, I miss more often than I should.

On short putts I like to see the ball roll purposefully into the centre of the cup, not dribble in via the side door. I believe that if you aim at the centre and hit the ball firmly, you'll hole out almost every time. You'll miss the odd one, sure, but it'll be the exception, not the rule.

If putts of this length give you grief, go to work on them. Line up a few short putts like this and attempt to hole each one in turn. If you miss one, start again from the beginning. This will sharpen up your holing out ability and get you used to seeing the ball roll into the hole – a huge psychological boost for your confidence.

Tony's Biography and Career Details

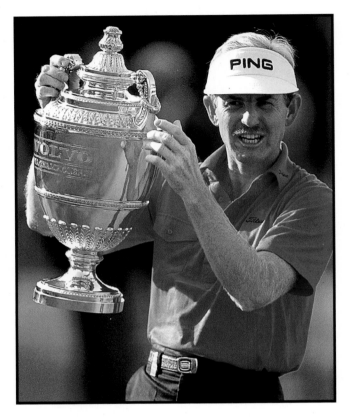

*Tony won the prestigious Volvo PGA Championship at Wentworth, Surrey,
in 1992, overcoming a field of the highest quality, which included Nick
Faldo, Jose Maria Olazabal, Bernhard Langer and Colin Montgomerie.
The victory earnt him a cheque for £100,000 and an invaluable
10-year exemption on the PGA European Tour.*

Full Name:
Anthony Alastair Johnstone

Nationality:
Zimbabwean

Date Of Birth:
2nd May, 1956

Height/weight:
5ft 8 1/2 ins (1.74 m);
10st 5lb (65.7 kgs)

Family:
Wife: Karen (married 1981);
Children: Dale (1985), Lauren (1990)

Interests:
Gardening, hunting,
Morgan cars

Turned Professional:
1979

Tournament Victories - 20

1984
South African Open
Charity Classic (SA)
South African Masters
Quinta Do Lago Portuguese Open
(Eur)

1986
Goodyear Classic (SA)

1987
ICL International (SA)
Minolta Copiers Matchplay (SA)
Wild Coast Classic (SA)

1988
ICL International (SA)
Minolta Copiers Matchplay (SA)
Bloemfontein Classic (SA)

1989
Lexington PGA (SA)

1990
Palabora Classic (SA)
Murphy's Cup (Eur)

1991
Murphy's Cup (Eur)

1992
Volvo PGA Championship (Eur)

1993
South African Masters (SA)
Zimbabwe Open
Philips South African Open

1994
Bell's Cup (SA)

Most people probably think that the photographic aspect of a golf instruction book is the easy part of the project. After all, the photographer just has to stand there, make sure the subject is in the centre of the viewfinder and then click away merrily, doesn't he? Unfortunately, it's not quite as simple as that.

Co-ordinating a five-day photoshoot is a major project and has to be carried out with military-like precision if you are to achieve the best results and stick to your schedule.

light offers the photographer a greater degree of flexibility and picture impact, I recommended postponement – a gamble which paid off when our back-up date fell in the middle of one of the best summers in history. Blessed with perfect light, I was able to fire off 10 frames of film per second. However, with Tony swinging the club at speeds approaching 70 mph, I'm sure you'll appreciate that there isn't much margin for error. Technically, ten frames per second still isn't fast enough to guarantee capturing impact, so I asked Tony to hit a minimum of three balls on each shot.

– Nick Walker.

ABOUT THE
PHOTOGRAPHY

Preparation is the key and the pre-planning of the photography took just as much time as the five-day session itself, if not more. In the few weeks prior to the shoot, I must have walked (or buggied) around the picturesque Brocket Hall golf course at least four or five times, making notes of the most suitable holes for the action shots. It's a wonderful golf course for scenic and instruction photography with wide, undulating fairways, spectator mounding, large bunkers and several interesting water holes.

I was looking specifically for locations which enabled me to make best use of the light, but which also had the clean, unobtrusive backdrops which would allow Tony to demonstrate his techniques without distractions, such as branches of trees creeping into the background.

However, what was an ideal hole for a down the line bunker play sequence, say, turned out to be totally unsuitable for face on putting. Finally, I selected just four or five holes and decided to work mainly around them.

The success of an outdoor photo shoot is dependent on the the light and our initial shoot was planned during unsettled weather. As sun-

Front cover
Photographed using a Nikon F90X body with a Nikkor 24 mm F2.8 lens and SB26 Flash. Taken at 1/3000 second at F4, plus fill in flash, using Kodak Panther X100 ISO film.

Overhead shots
All of the overhead pictures were taken using a Canon EOS 1N body fitted with a 20-35mm lens.

Close ups
All the close up shots, including the grips and lies, were photographed using a Canon EOS 1N body with a 28-70mm F2.8L lens.

Swing sequences
The majority of the swing sequences were photographed using a Canon EOS 1N RS body, fitted with a 200mm F1.8L lens. The only exception was the face on sequence of Tony playing a standard splash shot, which was shot using a 100mm F2 lens.
In each case, and firing at 10 frames per second, Tony was required to hit at least three shots from the same position to guarantee capturing impact and the critical swing positions.

Fuji Provia and Fuji Velvia film was used on all photos except for the front cover.

INDEX

(Captions are in italics)